FAD-FREE

MARKETING

A REAL-WORLD HANDBOOK FOR

RESTAURANTS

Bryan Duke

Candid Crest
Publishing

Fad-Free Marketing
A Real-World Handbook for Restaurants
Copyright © 2016 by Bryan Duke. All rights reserved
Candid Crest Publishing

ISBN-10: 1944947000
ISBN-13: 978-1944947002

THIS BOOK IS DEDICATED TO

The many pragmatic business managers who have had the courage to say "that doesn't seem to make sense" to a consultant or functional expert.

The marketing team at Procter & Gamble which strives to, and succeeds in, providing finer marketing training than that offered by most MBA programs.

Fad-Free Marketing

CONTENTS

Fad-Free Marketing

www.FadFreeMarketing.com

1

HOW TO USE THIS BOOK

As you've no doubt already discovered, there is a flood of information—both in print and online—about marketing. At the time of this printing, simple Amazon searches yielded more than eighty-five thousand books with the keyword "marketing" and nearly fifteen thousand books with the keyword "advertising." Google searches for the terms "advertising" and "marketing" yielded 2.5 billion results each.

Every day, countless books, articles, and blog posts are written about advertising and marketing. Some focus on small businesses, while others cater to marketing and product managers at large Fortune 500 firms. Some discuss specific and currently fashionable topics such as how to leverage buzz marketing through social media. Others highlight specific marketing tactics like search marketing or radio advertising. Some are about what to say to your customer and how to say it. Many seek to draw attention to (and often attempt to sell) specific advertising opportunities.

Talk about information overload.

Even marketing specialist professionals who spend their careers managing multimillion-dollar marketing budgets cannot hope to keep abreast of every new marketing strategy and tactic. Even they tend to rely on the assistance of advertising agencies or consultants.

But even relying on "experts" can be overwhelming.

According to the Bureau of Labor Statistics, as of 2008 there were about 50,100 advertising and public relations services in the United States, employing 462,300 wage and salary workers. (These are the advertising agency "Mad Men.") There are many thousands more independent advertising and marketing consultants, experts, and gurus. Some of these individuals are intelligent, thoughtful industry experts with decades of experience in the field. But, sadly, many more of the people who bill themselves as experts have little practical experience. Some are simply out to sell you a specific service, or collect hefty fees for little value. And most have never actually managed a business themselves.

Marketing in the Real World

Contrary to what marketing "professionals" would have you believe, small-business marketing in the real world rarely involves chasing after trends. It involves making some pretty basic decisions about the type of customer you want to attract and your sales pitch.

Then it involves spending relatively small sums of money on a few simple tactics, testing them, and continuing to invest in what works. Occasionally you may want to test a new approach but these tactics will rarely be new trends. They'll simply be new to your business. They'll be marketing tactics that many other businesses have already tried and there will be good information about how well they work and whether they may be right for you.

This book was written with this approach in mind. It was written to help the small business owner who isn't interested in chasing the latest marketing fad and who simply wants to understand the marketing fundamentals, and spend a little money to generate new customers in the most efficient and cost-effective way possible.

How This Book is Structured

First, rather than focusing on a specific marketing opportunity or the newest trend in marketing, this book takes you through the marketing fundamentals. We explain very simply and clearly what options are available to you and explain how to execute these options step-by-step. The sections are short and to the point and provide you with actionable tips to get started.

Second, we've provided very specific, real-life ideas that you can begin to implement tomorrow. We assume you don't have unlimited time to brainstorm and unlimited funds to test dozens of different marketing tactics that may or may not work for you. The ideas presented are specific and actionable. And, while we can't guarantee that all the ideas in this book will work for your specific business, they will, at a minimum, serve as much better thought-starters than the generic concepts many other marketing books and websites offer. Even if you already execute some of the tactics highlighted in this book, you may use the appropriate chapter to review your tactics for opportunities to improve the execution.

Keep a lookout for boxes like this one throughout the book. They contain very specific examples or ideas that you can try out immediately.

- Idea or Example 1
- Idea or Example 2
- Idea or Example 3

---

www.FadFreeMarketing.com

Third, because information changes rapidly, we've created a website with helpful and updated information, links, and specific vendor recommendations. The vendors that we recommend are not affiliated with our company. And, because you probably do not have the time or interest to vet many potential vendors, we try to limit the number of recommended resources to three or fewer good options in each tactical area. For example, if you want to design your own website quickly, we give you a few good resources on our own website that help you do that easily and inexpensively. And we'll update these resources as better or less expensive options become available.

While the information on our website is not required to implement any specific idea, it may help. The website serves simply as a supplement to the book, with information that can be updated as needed.

Finally, while you can develop a better feel for how to become an effective marketer by reading the full book, feel free to skip around as needed. We recommend reading at least the sections on targeting and messaging. These provide information that many business owners take for granted. The information here may seem simple, but many professional marketers—to their detriment—neglect aspects of these fundamentals every day. After reviewing this information, feel free to skip directly to sections of the book that highlight marketing tactics that interest you, or read through all of them for an overview of the different strategies and tactics available.

Marketing is one of those things that seems deceptively easy in theory but proves challenging in practice. You may already be doing a fine job of marketing in some respects, but there are always opportunities to improve your existing tactics, try more effective ones, target more profitable customers, or better manage your messaging so it's consistent and compelling.

We hope that you'll find this book helpful. Whether you do or don't, feel free to visit us online and tell us what information would make your job easier. We'll strive to provide it for you.

Book Sections

This book is divided into four core sections:

- **Targeting:** This section discusses your target audience. It will help you think about who you should be targeting with your marketing activities so that you have a better chance of reaching the type of person most likely to become a new and valuable customer.

- **Messaging:** We describe the importance of developing a crisp, clear, meaningful message for potential customers and focusing on delivering the message consistently across every touch point. We provide some ideas about what constitutes an effective message and how to develop one.

- **Marketing Tactics:** The majority of the book is dedicated to discussing specific marketing tactics, with a chapter highlighting each. We describe the tactic, why it may or may not be valuable to you, and how to get started. In many cases, we also provide you with specific ideas that will help you use that marketing vehicle more effectively, should you choose to. As mentioned, we also provide links on our website to resources that can help you with many of these tactics—focusing on a small number of vendors that do the job efficiently and effectively.

- **Measuring results:** This section provides a framework to help you determine the return on investment a particular marketing tactic has delivered.

2

TARGETING

Who are your customers? What do you know about them . . . really? What is the difference between the browser and a good customer who spends more time and money?

Understanding your best customers is the first step to attracting and creating more of them. The more you know about your customers, the more you'll know about how to reach similar potential customers. After all, if something about your offering appeals to a specific type of person—you simply need to tell more of the same types of people about your company and offering. Those are the people most likely to give you a shot.

You may already have a good idea of the types of people who buy from you—after all, you interact with them frequently. You know lots about them.

But do you know the right things and do you know what to do with that knowledge?

Demographics

While certain traits may be relatively obvious, like age, sex, or ethnicity, other traits are not as visually apparent, including marital status, number of people in the household, educational status, and income. These traits may be even more important in defining your customer than the more obvious traits.

All of these traits are referred to as demographic traits. These are the types of traits that are relatively easy to measure by census-takers and surveys and are therefore readily available from government sources. You can obtain these statistics for regions as small as specific zip codes. (Because they occasionally change, we've put links that help you better understand the demographics in your area on our website.)

It's important to understand the demographic characteristics of your ideal customer, because many marketing tactics are defined by the demographic group that they target. For example, a specific radio station may cater primarily to women of a certain income level and between the ages of twenty-five and thirty-five. If that audience matches your target customer, then advertising on that radio station could make sense.

Examples of demographic variables:

Take a look at your current customers (or, if your business is just beginning, your closest competitor's customers). How would you categorize your BEST customers using the following demographic criteria?

- Age (Typically expressed in terms of a range, such

---

as "Under 18," "25–35," or "65+." May also be expressed as a "generational cohort" such as "Millennials," "Gen-X," or "Baby Boomers.")

- Income (Also typically expressed as a range.)
- Sex
- Race (Why is this factor important in today's era of racial sensitivity? While it's true that all races are now much more represented across the spectrums of income, location, and other variables, it's also true that important cultural differences still exist. Certain messages, spokespeople, and offerings are more acceptable to specific races and cultures than others. Also, specific media properties may be of greater interest to specific groups.)
- Highest level of educational attainment (high school, college, graduate school, other)
- Home ownership (own, rent, live with parents)
- Employment status (This is not only whether someone is employed. This can also give you a sense of income and free time: full-time, part-time, evening shift, multiple jobs, etc.)
- Occupation
- Location (Typically, you'll be interested in specific neighborhoods or zip codes within a reasonable range of your business.)
- Marital status (Why should you care? Different things appeal to people in different life stages. Family-friendly messaging might appeal to households with kids but may actually be a turnoff for singles.)

- Urban category (typically urban, suburban, or rural)

Psychographics (Personality Traits)

Some traits are more difficult to capture than basic demographic information. Sometimes it's useful to group potential customers in terms of specific behaviors or psychological traits. These traits are known as psychographic variables and may include information about personality, hobbies, interests, lifestyle, and values. Often, these traits are even more important than demographic traits in understanding your customers and beginning to formulate a strategy to reach more people like them.

Obviously, every individual has many personality traits that define who he or she is, but as the owner/manager of a business that serves specific needs, you'll likely be interested in only a core few of them—those that are most relevant to your business and offerings.

To give you some sense of what these traits include and why they are important, it's useful to think about how some very different types of businesses may find psychographic information helpful:

- Outdoor landscapers, deck-builders, and similar businesses are probably interested in targeting homeowners with families. These are demographic traits. But let's go a bit deeper. They may specifically be interested in people who enjoy spending time outside but lack the ability or willingness to do home improvement work themselves. This is a psychographic trait. If it's true that a landscaper's best customers tend not to do their own landscaping, then posting a flyer in a Home Depot (a place frequented by many do-it-yourselfers), may not yield positive results. But getting the word out at a local lawn and garden show, where people are looking to pay for services, may work well. Or partnering with a handyman who already knows the types of people in the neighborhood who tend to hire professionals rather than doing work themselves may be a sound strategy.

- Investment managers might be interested in people of a certain net worth (a demographic trait) but may also be interested in the types of people who trust expert opinion more than they trust their own ability to manage their wealth (a psychographic trait). While it may be simple to target zip codes with high-net-worth residents or target magazines that appeal to high-net-worth individuals, many competitors may advertise there already. But an investment manager who understands that his or her best customers don't trust their own ability to manage money may find more creative ways to reach them. Perhaps these people are more likely to watch television shows or read magazines with specific investment advice. Or perhaps they don't trust their own abilities because they've experienced problems in the past. The savvy investment advisor may be able to combine a list of customers who have filed for bankruptcy some time ago with those that currently have a high level of income or net worth. These people may now have money to invest but may be less willing to trust themselves to invest it.

- Restaurants may be interested in people with certain levels of disposable income (demographic trait) but are probably also interested in the types of people who like to dine away from home and have a certain culinary adventurousness (psychographic trait). Knowing this, it may make sense to partner with a local travel agency—particularly one that caters to a region that matches the restaurant's theme/menu.

As these examples demonstrate, your ideal customer will share a combination of demographic and psychographic traits that may be useful to you. Those combinations may help you identify both traditional and more unusual opportunities to reach new customers just like them.

So, demographic and psychographic traits are both important. However, psychographic traits may say more about a person's likelihood to become a customer—and therefore may be more important to you—than demographic traits. While your customers may share certain demographic traits, and these traits may help you select the most appropriate advertising vehicle to reach them, it's their psychological traits that drive behaviors.

For example, while many BMW buyers are of a certain financial status, it's a love of performance vehicles and an interest in prestige that tend to drive them to purchase a BMW versus another premium automobile. Income may help the manager of a BMW dealership determine what magazine to advertise in, but shared psychology helps craft the message and may help identify other unique advertising opportunities.

Examples of potentially important psychographic variables for restaurants:

The following are specific types of psychographic information that might help you identify commonalities among your customers that enable you to better target them. For example, if you know you appeal to the business traveler on an expense account, you may begin to target them directly through local hotels and generate specific offers that help to differentiate your business:

Social Preferences	Some people are more comfortable dining alone or in small groups. Others prefer a social atmosphere and people-watching. Is your restaurant intimate or more open and social? Be sure to reflect this appropriately in your messaging so you attract customers in the right frame of mind.
Entertainment Preferences	Do you feature entertainment of any kind including music, performances, or even unique artwork? Consider getting the message out in the types of environments that feature similar artists or enthusiasts of the artist or performers. Or consider partnering with the artist/entertainers themselves.
Health Conscious	Do you cater to people who appreciate healthy dining options, count calories, are vegetarian or vegan, prefer fresh, never-frozen foods, gluten-free or other health

	requirements? Consider partnering with shows, publications, and events that cater to similar interests.
Expense Accounts	Does your restaurant appeal to those entertaining clients or even traveling alone on an expense account? Where else might you reach people that are traveling? Hotels? Rental Car Companies?
Environment Appeal	Think about the types of people that your décor appeals to. Do you have a comfortable, homey establishment, a contemporary environment, an upscale restaurant with a rich décor, a restaurant of historical significance or of architectural note? Is yours a simple concept that simply serves good meals at reasonable prices? How can you more specifically reach these types of people? If décor is central to who you are, how can you reach diners who are most likely to appreciate it?
Early Morning/Late Nighters	Specific types of people prefer to dine at specific times of day. These preferences may be driven by occupation, age, family commitments, social or lifestyle preferences, entertainment habits, etc. How do you reach those types of people? Also, consider advertising at certain times of day. If yours is a late-night place, an

	advertisement on the radio at midnight might remind those driving home from a bar or late shift to stop by and grab a bite on their way home.
Family First	Some diners prefer to dine with the whole family on certain occasions. If you cater to families, consider getting the message out in family-friendly environments or targeting family-friendly events or places. (e.g. schools, parks, sporting events, etc.)
Status-Seekers	These diners may be enticed by rare or unique offerings, special treatment, famous patrons, or up-scale décor. They may seek opportunities to impress guests or simply to experience something worthy of a story. Perks and status-symbols appeal to these diners, as does the potential to tell an enviable story. (I sat next to XYZ at dinner this evening and had a terrific conversation.)

Is Your Current Customer Your Ideal Customer?

So you've looked at your current customer (or the customers of your closest or more well-established competition, if your business is still in the start-up phase). Before proceeding with this information, it's worth asking whether your *current* customer represents your *ideal* customer.

If you've been in business for a while, it's likely that customers who are most interested in your services have discovered you, either directly or by referral. Even if this is the case, there are still opportunities to use this knowledge to enhance revenue and profit. Determining what your best customers look like and offering incentives to them may help you retain these valuable customers by ensuring their loyalty. But, if you're reading this book, chances are you're also interested in attracting new customers.

If your business is relatively new, or if you're considering adding a new product or service, you may want to re-examine your current customer base. It's possible that a certain type of customer would be even more interested in your company and potentially more profitable to you—either because they may become more frequent customers or because they may spend more.

A questionnaire is an excellent way to learn more about your current customers. A well-crafted one that focuses on actionable information can tell you a lot of things that you may not already know. We talk more specifically about how to structure a good questionnaire in chapter three. The questionnaire warrants its own section because it can help you with both targeting and messaging (discussed in chapter two).

Be Focused

Hopefully, the information you've collected defines a relatively narrow group of customers. If the information is too broad, it will be less useful.

An Italian restaurant doesn't just want diners who

like Italian food. It may be interested specifically in somewhat sophisticated, worldly couples who enjoy a moderately priced wine with dinner. A real-estate agent obviously is interested in customers who want to purchase homes, but he or she may also have chosen to specialize in young couples with a good rental history who do not yet have children but who are interested in purchasing a first home in an area with lots of bars and restaurants or with easy access to downtown.

The more specific you can be about your target audience, the easier it will be to reach the right customer. (Again, we'll tell you what to do with this information later.)

Primary Target vs. Secondary Target

Hopefully, you're able to identify what your best existing and potential customers look like. These are your ideal, most profitable customers—the ones you want to pursue relentlessly because they will help drive the best business results. In marketing circles, this is known as your primary target, also sometimes called your "prime prospect."

Other groups of customers may also be important to you for different reasons. Perhaps this is because you've added a new offering to your business that attracts a slightly different type of customer (e.g., a house painter has added gutter cleaning services to his offerings or a gas station/convenience store has added a small sandwich shop on the property). Or, perhaps your offering appeals to two groups of customers for very different reasons. (A craft store may generate significant revenue from people who do lots of crafts, but may also generate revenue from interior designers or grade-school art teachers.) These types of customers are collectively known as your "secondary target" and may be important sources of additional revenue.

Presumably, you have a limited marketing budget. Therefore, it's important to decide which of these customer groups you want to spend money talking to. Typically, you'll derive the most revenue and profit from your primary target, but you may decide that you've reached nearly as many of those customers as you can. This is a concept known as "penetration." If roughly 80 percent of the people who represent your primary target in your area are already customers, then perhaps focusing your efforts on a secondary target might provide a better marketing return. Doing this may be easier than reaching the few remaining people who constitute your primary target.

Or it may be possible to extract even more revenue from your primary target. Many times it is easier to deepen your relationship with a customer who already likes you than to seek entirely new customers.

Purchase Funnel

This book is focused primarily on how to obtain new customers for your business. Companies that engage in marketing activity aimed at acquiring new customers are focused on "awareness and trial-driving" strategies.

But driving awareness or trial are not the only activities you can engage in to grow your business. There are many opportunities to try and capture more revenue or prevent it from leaving.

One of the simplest ways to visualize all of these different opportunities is with a "Purchase Funnel."

Marketing agencies and consultants have come up with a thousand ways of presenting this and laying it out, but we present a simple one on the next page.

Because your marketing efforts are typically designed to make more people aware of your business, this shows up on the top of the funnel. Essentially, your marketing investment is what fills the funnel with potential customers by making more customers aware of your business.

From awareness, a natural cascade begins.

Not everyone that hears about your business will be interested, for whatever reason. Distance may be an issue. The timing may not be right. Your service may not be what they're looking for at this time. In other words, many of the people who you reach with your marketing efforts will not be in your primary target set. They're not right for you and you may not be right for them. You'll simply agree not to date and move on.

Those that are within your targeted group may reach the next stage called the "consideration" stage. They're interested but haven't yet had an opportunity to try you. Your marketing efforts can also appeal to this group of people with what are called "trial-driving strategies." Maybe a gentle reminder on the radio as they're driving home or a billboard might be enough to get them to take the next step. Maybe a discount or special offer of some sort would help.

The next stage is the "trial" stage. A new customer has finally decided to give you a shot. If they have a great experience, hopefully they'll "repeat", and repeat again, until eventually they move to the final stage in the funnel and become "loyal customers"

Purchase Funnel

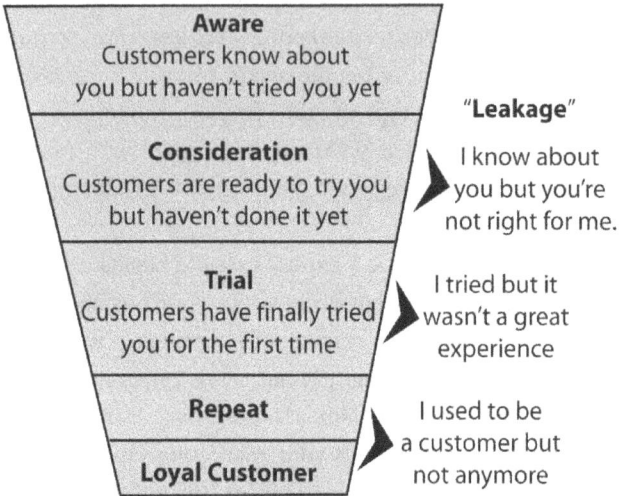

Aware
Customers know about you but haven't tried you yet

Consideration
Customers are ready to try you but haven't done it yet

Trial
Customers have finally tried you for the first time

Repeat

Loyal Customer

"**Leakage**"

I know about you but you're not right for me.

I tried but it wasn't a great experience

I used to be a customer but not anymore

This process is presented as a funnel because the number of customers who move from one stage to the next becomes progressively smaller until you're left with a relatively small percentage of loyal users.

Potential customers "leak" from the funnel at different stages for different reasons. There are general strategies for each step along the way.

- Awareness: Potential customers may become aware of you through marketing & advertising. However, they may not consider you because your business isn't right for them for whatever reason.

- Consideration: Targeting the right people will ensure that more of them are the types of people who will actually consider becoming a customer. This will also make your marketing spend more efficient. The primary intent of this chapter is to ensure that you know the types of people you should be talking to in order to help ensure you're not wasting time and money talking to people that will never consider your company. However, even if a potential customer would consider you, they may not actually get around to it for a variety of reasons.

- Trial: To get more of the "consideration" customers to actually purchase from you involves "trial-driving strategies." We discuss these more in the marketing tactics sections later in the book. People are habitual and sometimes require incentives or very good reasons to break out of their routines and/or try something new. The general strategy is to combine a great single-minded message at the right time and possibly with the right added incentive.

- Repeat: Once a customer agrees to try, the resulting experience will determine if they come back. You can also encourage them to come back with incentives, discounts or additional communication.

- Loyal: Hopefully customers will come back so often that they become "loyalists," which constitute your most valued customers. These types of customers are also the most likely to tell other people about you, providing you with some free advertising in the process. Delivering the best experience to these customers is not the focus of this book, but there are opportunities to retain them, such as offering incentives at the right time or increasing the amount of money they spend. We highlight some of these opportunities below.

It may be easier and less costly to sell additional products or services to existing customers. And, in the process, it may make your existing customers even more loyal, as they learn they simply can't do without you. As they spend more of their category dollars with you, it may make them even less likely to consider the competition. (Why bother when they can get everything they need from your business?)

As with your primary message, the simplest way to discover how to retain your existing customers, or determine what they might be willing to spend more money on, is to ask them. Or ask a competitor's customers, if you're still in the process of opening your business.

Examples of strategies and the types of messaging that can help retain existing customers and obtain more revenue from them:

- Increase offering range (thereby increasing the share of dollars spent with you as opposed to your competition):
    - Expand your hours (breakfast, lunch, dinner, late-night). Make sure people know about it.
    - Ensure that a course besides your main course is "must have." For example, ensure that customers can't pass up your famous ice-cream burrito for dessert. And, be sure to advertise the offering to drive awareness! Partner with a local DJ who loves the special and get him talking.
    - Offer restaurant memorabilia. It drives

---

revenue as it drives awareness via free advertising! The best memorabilia are most likely to be shown to others (clothing) or is reminiscent of a house specialty (e.g. The Soup House Soup Bowl).

o Enable people to order take-out or consider delivery. Consider partnering with one of the large delivery organizations to be considered among their broad range of partners or risk losing a potential sale to a competitor who is listed.

o Sell items related to your ambiance (e.g. music, art, particularly notable furnishings, unique eating utensils or flatware, etc.). Starbucks does this well.

o Offer catering for additional revenue and to expose more people to your menu items.

• Increase value:

o Offer and drive awareness of up-scale dining options.

o Offer and appropriately price a particularly fresh or local-sourced option.

o Partner with a celebrity chef, local non-food celebrity, or other figure to create a special offering that's worth more to someone who is a fan.

o Include limited-time offers (other than daily specials) that drive interest and excitement. These could be specials of the month or seasonal specialties.

o Feature a unique, exotic food that few have

ever heard of and that the diner cannot find anywhere else.

o Offer special VIP seating options to those willing to pay for the privilege.

o Consider a special guest celebrity night or opportunity to dine with a celebrity in a more intimate setting.

o Provide an opportunity to dine with the chef or owner.

o Host special events that appeal to specific individuals who want to mingle with other, similar people.

- Increase top-of-mind (among existing customers in ways OTHER than traditional advertising):

  o Ensure your existing diners think of you more often by giving them small useful items to take home that serve as regular reminders (magnets, matches, wet-naps that they may keep in a drawer or a car, etc.).

  o Send them home with a calendar of events.

  o Sell a cookbook.

How do you know which general area of the purchase funnel to focus on? In an ideal world, you'd have a sense for how you compare to a typical company or a key competitor. However, since benchmarking is fairly difficult, you'll have to make an assumption for what needs improvement and focus there.

Now What?

Hopefully, going through the exercise of identifying and better understanding your target audience will help you find some new and potentially profitable opportunities to reach more of them. It may even help you refine your current business model or drive greater focus.

Ensuring that you understand the most important and actionable specifics about your customers will enable you to craft messages that directly appeal to them and to reach more people like them through targeted marketing activities. Ensuring that your employees understand who your best customers are—and treat them particularly well—will help earn more referrals, which will attract even more people just like them.

Targeting Summary

- Understanding your best customers can help you attract more people just like them.
- Demographic data includes factual, "survey" type of information, like sex, age, and income, and can help you select appropriate marketing vehicles based on who they target.
- Psychographic data include psychological information, such as attitudes and behaviors of your target audience, and can help you craft a compelling message or seek out new, unusual, and potentially very targeted advertising vehicles to reach them.

- Your primary target consists of the customers who are most likely to purchase your primary offering in the greatest numbers. You may also have a less important secondary target which may represent a source of revenue for you but should not distract from your pursuit of your primary target.

3

MESSAGING

If you had only thirty seconds to talk to a potential customer in your prime prospect group (see previous section for more information on targeting), how would you convince them to try your business? This is the root of the challenge you'll face when deciding exactly what information to include in your marketing efforts.

If you had ten minutes or more, you'd probably have a much better chance of selling them on your business. Unfortunately, you rarely have an opportunity to talk to more than a few potential customers for this long. You've got a business to run, with hundreds of details to attend to, which simply doesn't leave you much time to talk directly to potential customers. In short, you're often too busy dealing with the customers you've already got.

Traditional marketing vehicles (billboards, radio, online text ads, etc.) will reach many more customers than you ever could individually. Unfortunately, most marketing vehicles do not provide you with an opportunity to have the in-depth conversation you'd like to have with a potential customer. You need to begin thinking of a story that convinces in seconds not minutes.

A Concise Message

The next time you're in the car, pay close attention to a radio advertisement. Most radio ads are purchased in thirty-second increments. This may seem like a long time until you realize how little "substance" there is in a good radio ad. If an ad isn't interesting to you, you're likely to switch to another station. Or (more likely), you'll simply ignore it. For this reason, a good radio advertisement is often entertaining as well as informative. It has to catch your attention and hold it.

Often, the entertaining element of the ad takes a good chunk of time out of the thirty seconds. Imagine writing down every word of the actual script of the radio advertisement. It might not even amount to a good-sized paragraph. And much of that text serves only to entertain or set up the idea without actually selling whatever the business has to offer. The actual sales pitch will likely be only a sentence or two.

Some advertisements dispense with the entertainment value entirely and try to pack as much of the "pitch" into the ad as possible, replacing entertainment with sheer volume. (Car dealerships are famous for this.) How much of this information would you guess the average listener actually absorbs? How many people could tell you anything about the advertisement five minutes after hearing it? Not many.

Why? Because catching the attention of your potential customer can be nearly as important as delivering a compelling message. Cramming all sorts of important information into an ad is of little value if the customer has tuned out (literally or figuratively). Beyond the fact that an information-packed advertisement is probably not entertaining or interesting enough to hold your attention, it's also trying to do too much. The information that may be of actual interest to you is lost somewhere in an overly verbose sales pitch, full of information you're not very interested in.

This is true regardless of the advertising medium, radio, television, billboards, or anything else.

The advertisers who try to include twenty messages in one advertisement aren't focusing on the one or two things most important to you. This is probably because they aren't sure what those things are and what will catch your attention. So they decide to throw everything into the advertisement. Or, they believe that because different people like different things, everything should go into the ad so that it appeals to all people equally.

Even very experienced companies can make these common mistakes if they haven't taken the time to understand and really focus on what's truly important to the primary target. Let's talk about how you can do better.

Prioritize

Steve Jobs was quoted as saying, "The most important decisions you make are not the things you do, but the things you decide not to do." You've probably heard similar truisms as applied to management.

This wisdom applies to marketing as well. The most difficult part of developing a marketing message is not deciding what to say—it's deciding what NOT to say, or at least deciding what to relegate to a lesser priority.

Even if a particular marketing vehicle provides you with room to include lots of information about your business, like an e-mail, a flyer, or a website (any of which allows you to include paragraphs of information), you still have to decide what message you'd like to focus on first and most prominently. This priority message might become your headline, or it might manifest itself as a large picture on your advertisement (or both).

Imagine you're walking through a shopping mall parking lot. Upon approaching your car, you see two sales flyers tucked beneath the windshield wiper. You notice that both feature a picture of a shiny new Roadster and some text.

Sales Flyer 1	Sales Flyer 2
GIANT AUTOMOTIVE TENT SALE !!!	The NEW 20XXX Roadster With Autodrive is Here !!!

Sales Flyer 1

GIANT AUTOMOTIVE
TENT SALE !!!

Murphy's Cars
This Sunday
August 15th
Find Great Deals on the
20XX Roadster
with Autodrive

Sales Flyer 2

The NEW
20XXX Roadster
With Autodrive
is Here !!!

Murphy's Cars
is celebrating with a
Giant Automotive
Tent Sale
This Sunday
August 15th

Notice that the actual words used are nearly identical but the focus is much different. Both talk about a sale and a specific model of new car with "autodrive."

Flyer 1 is clearly focused on the sale, assuming that the idea of a discount on a new car is what motivates buyers. Flyer 2 is focused on the availability of the car itself and the hot new autodrive feature. It assumes that the car and the feature are what will attract buyers. The tent sale is simply an added incentive.

Which advertisement do you believe is more appealing?

The answer depends on whether the target customer is motivated by the prospect of saving money or by the prospect of being one of the first to inspect and possibly own a brand new model year vehicle. If the roadster falls into the luxury class of vehicles, then the second concept might be more appealing. However, if the roadster is a value car that appeals to first-time car buyers, then the idea of saving money might be more important.

Of course, the "tent sale" message in the first flyer has become so generic that potential buyers may have glossed right over it. Saving money, while important, is not always the most interesting or compelling information about a particular product or business.

This example illustrates that the same information can be presented in two very different ways to appeal to different types of customers. (In this case, value shoppers vs. luxury buyers or early adopters.)

Primary and Secondary Benefits

The most important message is also called your primary message or primary benefit. It's the one benefit you offer your customer that is most likely to appeal to him or her. Or, it could simply be the message that most differentiates you in the market.

Consider Walmart. Most shoppers associate Walmart primarily with low prices because "everyday low prices" has become the retailer's area of focus. But there are many other things the retailer could have chosen to communicate through marketing. Imagine these alternative positioning ideas:

- Walmart: The largest selection under one roof.
- Walmart: Your product, in stock when you need it.
- Walmart: Service with a smile.
- Walmart: Always open for business (24/7/365)

Arguably, Walmart could have chosen to focus its messaging on any one of these areas. However, the retailer decided price would be the primary benefit and its primary means of differentiation. At that point, everything else, including store size, selection, location, service, and so on, became secondary benefits.

The company realized two important things:

First, and perhaps obviously, price was important to shoppers. While not all shoppers are concerned with price for all products, enough are that the company has become not only the largest retailer but (as of 2016) the largest public company by revenue in the world. Price was so important to customers, and comparison shopping such a hassle, that Walmart decided it would take price out of the equation entirely. The perception most shoppers share is that when you shop at Walmart, you're guaranteed the lowest price.

Secondly, and perhaps even more importantly, the company saw an opportunity to differentiate itself in an area where it could win. Walmart, with its scale, its incredibly efficient inventory management system, and its market power over suppliers, is uniquely positioned to win on price. Witness the decline of K-Mart, which attempted to go head-to-head with the Bentonville giant, and witness the decision of Target to (some would say more wisely) cede the absolute price position to its larger competitor and focus instead on product selection, enabling it to appeal to a different customer who appreciates fun and affordable style.

Consider these other examples and imagine how each of these companies might have been very different had it chosen to focus on any one of its secondary benefits instead. Also, notice that each of the decisions to focus on a specific primary benefit was probably driven by the area in which the company had a right to win versus its competition.

Company/ Product	Primary Benefit/ Focus Area	Secondary Benefits/ Could Have Focused On:
Subway	healthy fast food	taste, convenience, value, location
Disney	family entertainment	education, excitement, cultural exposure, cartoons
Federal Express	overnight delivery	broad distribution network, careful handling, customer service, tracking software, logistics
Verizon	broad, reliable coverage	price, phone/device variety, customer service
Volvo	safety	performance, reliability, features, luxury
MTV	trendsetting youthful entertainment	informative social news, fashion, music
Rolex	premium timepieces	fashion, cutting-edge technology

Two Primary Messages?

You may have realized that many of the above primary benefits include two ideas. For example, Subway's healthy fast food benefit actually has two concepts embedded in one idea: the idea of healthy and the acknowledgement that the restaurant competes in the quick service restaurant category (fast). For Subway, the key differentiator is "healthy," but the chain can really only claim this benefit when compared to those within its competitive set, which includes fast-food burger chains. In this context, Subway is not defining its competitive set as Whole Foods or a local salad bar.

To avoid confusion and to point out that the companies listed actually do have a primary focus, we've underlined the single word that best represents the primary benefit.

You may already know what category Subway and the other companies on the list play in because Subway has already spent many millions of dollars establishing its brand and the category. This same approach may not work for your company which is not yet a household name.

With that in mind, you may have to tell people a bit more about yourself, including what business category you compete in. Even longstanding regional businesses may be unknown to area newcomers or those who have no previous experience with the category and are just beginning to shop around. To a customer who doesn't know better, "Tabbard Brothers—Excellent Service for 100 Years," could refer to a restaurant, a home builder, a landscaper, a law firm, or almost anything.

Always ensure that it's clear to customers what category you play in before seeking to differentiate yourself with your primary message.

Your Primary Benefit

Listed below are some thought-starters you might consider using as a primary point of differentiation versus your competition. This list does not and cannot include everything. There may be something very unique to your business that isn't captured here. Think in terms of what your competition already offers, what's important to your customer and potential customers, and what gives you a unique right to win.

Ideally, your primary benefit should be something your competition will find difficult to duplicate or surpass.

Thought-starters and examples of primary (or secondary) benefits for restaurants:
• Food-related:
• Most authentic or the best ethnic cuisine
• Vegetarian
• Meal specialty (best brunch, specialty pastries, broad selection of oysters)
• Locally sourced
• Good wine list
• Ambiance:
• Outdoor space or view
• Architecture
• Artwork (specialty, updated, local)

- "See and be seen"/social
- Quiet/intimate
- Luxurious
- Star sighting or people watching
- Historically significant
- Good single scene
- Reminiscent of a particular place/transporting experience (e.g. Just like visiting Brazil)
- Trendy
- Specialty Appeal:
  - Family-friendly
  - Budget conscious
  - Early-bird specials
  - Chef's table or chef's events
  - Business dining
  - Prix Fixe
  - Late dining
- Other:
  - Eclectic or quirky mood
  - Friendly owners or particularly friendly service
  - Parking (if unusual in your area) or valet parking specifically
  - Private rooms
  - Big party friendly
  - Catering
  - Pre-theater
  - Tea service
  - Featured in a movie, book, local review

- Landmark status
- Convenient to a landmark or special location (near the ballpark, museum, busy highway exit)

Message Consistency

Once you've determined what your primary benefit and message should be, it's important to communicate this message consistently so that existing and new customers always know what you stand for. This is particularly important if you're reaching out to potential new customers or those who don't know much about you but it also serves as an important and constant reminder of what you stand for in a confusing and ever-changing marketplace.

Returning to the Walmart example, imagine the temptation to stray away from the core "lowest price" message. Shouldn't Walmart attempt to defend against Target stores by stocking and advertising more "up-market" inventory items? Shouldn't Walmart compete with Amazon by broadening its product offering and moving aggressively into the online space? While Walmart has made moves in each of these areas (the Martha Stewart collection and Walmart.com are examples), the company continues to compete very effectively and primarily on price. It already "owns" this primary benefit, and any move in another direction risks losing this focus.

Walmart is consistent. The low-price concept dominates everything it does. Excluding the occasional public service advertisement, its marketing message is almost entirely focused on price. For a time, the retailer featured employees in its advertising. The idea was that Walmart was so focused on saving money so that it could offer you the lowest prices that it wouldn't even pay professional actors – even though it could clearly afford to. Product pricing dominates in-store signs. The company offers a low-price guarantee. The company sends the signal that it saves money for shoppers with stores that look like warehouses and even a squat, brick corporate headquarters that hardly looks like the gleaming glass and steel office tower one might expect of the world's largest company by revenue. Visitors to the company's HQ must even purchase their own coffee in the waiting area. Meetings take place in rooms separated by accordion-style folding wall separators like you might find in a neighborhood community center. In short, the company lives, breathes, and constantly communicates its key benefit in everything it does.

Competitors with the Same Message

What if one or several competitors start highlighting the same primary message you've chosen as your differentiator?

What would the marketing managers at Subway do if a national fast-food franchise began competing by selling deli sandwiches or healthier options? What would the managers at Volvo do if Honda, Toyota, and BMW started touting product safety?

In a competitive marketplace, there will always be changes in competitive messaging. A competitor may decide it has a greater right to own a particular benefit than you do. Perhaps your competitor is trying to siphon off some of your customer base and believes it can do so by neutralizing your perceived advantage. Perhaps your competition is simply desperate.

Before you rush off to change your advertising and the tagline on your business card, consider the equity that you've already built in your core message and the potential confusion that might result from changing what you stand for.

For years, Metamucil dominated the market for fiber supplements, until Benefiber came along and introduced a clear, tasteless fiber that dissolved completely in a glass of water. The advertising promised a much easier way to get your required daily serving of fiber. The marketing managers on Metamucil had to decide what the brand would stand for in the face of this new competitive threat. Would it talk to consumers about its taste, or would it perhaps highlight greater efficacy?

Your primary message in most cases should match your primary strategy. Your message is the articulation of the differentiating principle you've built your business around. Therefore, changing your message isn't necessarily a simple exercise. Walmart has invested so heavily in being the low-price leader that it's very unlikely the company will change its marketing message in the short run—even when competition attempts to highlight the same message. Instead, Walmart has chosen to aggressively assert its low-price credentials by pressuring its suppliers to slash prices and pushing its store managers to shop the competition to ensure their prices are the lowest on every item, every day, guaranteed. There have been instances in which store managers have slashed prices to compete with a local upstart several times, finally dropping them well below the product purchase price and holding them there to send a message to the local competition that Walmart will not be beaten on price—ever.

Faced with a competitive message that's similar or superior to your own, there are a couple of options you might consider:

Stay the course. It's difficult to imagine the makers of Cap'n Crunch cereal abandoning their "stays crunchy in milk" positioning and beginning to highlight the cereal's nutritional value simply because a competitor introduced a "crunchier" cereal. If you've worked hard to ensure that you have a better offering in a particular category, own it with pride! Changing your messaging can result in confusion and may even result in customers' assuming your competitor really does have a better offering than you do.

You might consider telling people why you have the better offering. At the same time, you should probably invest in ensuring that you actually do have the best offering in your chosen area of superiority. You might cite supporting facts or customer testimonials in your advertising. You could dial up your investment in marketing temporarily to ensure customers don't forget about your superior offering. This may also send a signal to competition that you're not about to back down.

One note of caution—think carefully before you make direct competitive comparisons in your advertising. This can often backfire in two ways: First, many people do not like negative advertising. What may work for politicians may not work for a business that must earn its customer's vote over and over again. In an extreme case, it may even result in a competitive challenge or lawsuit. Second, why drive awareness of your competitor's business by mentioning it in your advertisement? That's free publicity! You may think you're giving the public a reason to avoid your competitor, but you may also have ensured that your competitor's business stays top of mind. Customers may remember your competitor's name but not the negative message itself! A Procter and Gamble study in the 1990s found that, on average, advertisements that highlighted a competitor in a negative light drove awareness of the competitive product, but had very little overall impact on customers' intent to purchase the competing product.

Evolve. Some benefits are very difficult to own. Price is a good example. If you've staked a position as a low-price leader, you'll find yourself constantly defending your turf, as many of your competitors will offer sales or trial offers to generate business. There's often so much noise when it comes to price, deals, and specials that, with the exception of Walmart, it's nearly impossible for one business to offer the lowest price all the time. If it seems like everyone is focused on a particular benefit, you may want to consider focusing on something else. Other reasons you may choose to change your messaging include a change in business strategy, new business offerings, a change in location, or new management with a new focus.

Messaging Summary

- Ensure your message is concise and to the point.
- Prioritize your most important message and communicate it consistently.

- Choose a primary benefit that enables you to define yourself versus your competition clearly in customers' minds.
- Don't waste much time and money talking about other things your business has to offer.
- Make sure any advertising message highlights your primary benefit.
- Don't change your message unless you have a very good reason to do so.

4

THE QUESTIONAIRE OR SURVEY

You probably know, or can easily gather information about your customers, competitors, and impressions about your business yourself. But sometimes the direct approach is best. For those questions that you're not certain about or would like to confirm, it may be easiest to simply ask your customers yourself.

There are several broad types of questions you may want to ask that each help with specific objectives.

- Target Audience: Some questions help you understand your best customers better, including how you might attract more of them.

- Messaging: Some questions help you determine what your primary benefit is in the eyes of your customers, how you're differentiated from your competitors.

- Offering: Some questions help you refine your offering.

- All of the above: A well-crafted question can often help you answer several of the above at once.

You could ask some customers these types of questions yourself or ask your employees to do so for you, but providing your customers with a formal survey ensures that they have time to answer the questions themselves and also provides you with a record of their answers that you can evaluate in a group. This will help you to establish trends and commonalities more easily.

Surveys can take the form of simple paper surveys or you might provide a link to a website that will tally the responses for you. Our website has some helpful links.

You may want to provide customers with an incentive to answer your questions which may encourage more to do so. However, in some cases you may specifically choose not to "pay" customers to fill out your survey so that only those customers who are most interested in giving you their opinion will do so.

Bear in mind that the types of customers who take the time to fill out a survey typically do so because they have something specific to say (either positive or negative).

If a consumer has filled out a survey simply to complain about something specific, this isn't necessarily a bad result. It may give you an opportunity to learn about an issue that you may never otherwise know about, and it may help to defuse a situation by giving your customer an outlet to vent their frustrations. However, the remainder of their answers may or may not be particularly relevant to what you're trying to accomplish.

Surveys should be relatively short. This is primarily because many customers are willing to answer a few questions about your business but few will be willing to invest more than ten minutes. A good survey should include between five and ten questions to encourage the greatest level of engagement. Clearly, you'll need to be very selective in the types of questions you include.

Examples of some useful survey questions:	
These questions can help you understand your customers and can also help to refine your offering and your messaging by determining what diners like most about your restaurant. These questions are designed to help you get the greatest "bang for the buck."	
Example Question	**Why ask this?**
How often do you dine with us?	This question will enable you to divide all of your questionnaires into two stacks: one that consists of your best customers, whose answers are most valuable in helping you attract more customers just like them, and a second that consists of customers who may not be perfect fits for your restaurant, or who may help you identify opportunities for increased sales.
What do you like best about our restaurant?	This helps you determine what to focus on in your messaging (your primary benefit) and tells

	you something about your customers' preferences in the process.
Do you tend to plan ahead or tend to visit us more spontaneously or last minute?	If more customers plan ahead, you may want to reach them through reservation, review, or ratings websites or magazines. If they're more spontaneous, consider radio or billboard ads that catch them while they're on the road or in the neighborhood.
What type of entertainment do you prefer while dining? How important is this to you?	Ask this only if it's relevant for your restaurant. The answers can not only help you select entertainment, but if it's truly important, you may even choose to highlight it in your advertising, or partner with relevant artists to help get the word out.
What items would you like to see on our menu?	Even better than asking what menu items consumers like best (which you probably already know), this forces consumers to think up new offerings for you and says a lot about their interests. Are your customers passionate about fresh food? Do they love dessert or are they focused on drinks and appetizers? Sometimes answers will surprise you by focusing on

	features like price which may say something about how value-conscious your diners are. Suggestions may include lots of sharable options, which may indicate that your restaurant encourages lots of social interaction or attracts people when they're in a particularly social mood.
What one feature of our restaurant would you change?	Similar to the menu question above, this can help you refine your service but also says a lot about your customers. What do they value? Do they make comments about lighting? This may say something about who they dine with and why they visit. Do they comment on parking, entertainment?
Who do you tend to dine here with?	If you don't already know, this can help to establish the types of groups your restaurant appeals to. Do you attract work groups or business people entertaining clients? Perhaps you should distribute information to local businesses or cater to them at a discount to establish awareness and interest. Do you attract groups of friends, families,

	mainly couples, or even singles? This information can help you establish which groups to reach out to.
How did you first learn about our restaurant?	This can help you do a better job of reaching potential customers when they're most receptive. It also may say a lot about who might be talking about you already and in what forums.
Besides us, what is your favorite restaurant?	The answer to this question may surprise you. A consistent answer here will help to identify your closest competitor and in turn can help you determine what features might be worth highlighting to help you differentiate. At the same time, this may also help you identify what your customer really like about both restaurants by understanding the similarities between the two. Finally, this may not be a competitor at all – it may simply be a "complimentary" restaurant (for example a good brunch restaurant that compliments your terrific dinner offerings). Of course, if you were considering offering brunch, this restaurant

	might be a good one to emulate.
What could we do to encourage you to dine with us more often?	Sometimes there's no substitute for being direct. This question helps you understand what you can do better, but is positioned to encourage your customer to offer a constructive answer rather than simply complaining about service or price. Should you do more of the same, or do you need to change course? If you can deliver on this need or something similar, then you've just discovered a great benefit to feature in advertising to encourage more customers to dine with you more often.

When reviewing the results, separate your best customers from the rest, as mentioned above. From this you'll develop a "profile" of your best customers and will be in a better position to find more people just like them.

On the other hand, the survey results from customers who are NOT your best customers can help you identify a few things. First, it may help you understand opportunities to improve your offering. Second, because you can't be all things to all people, it may help you learn more about the types of people who are not necessarily the best fit for your business. This can also help you determine if some of your marketing efforts are being wasted against the types of people who may not become your best customers.

We've provided links to specific questionnaire

resources on our website.

AN INTRODUCTION TO MARKETING TACTICS

There are many ways to reach a potential customer with a message about your business. None is inherently superior to any other, but some will be more appropriate for your business, given your strategy, situation, and target audience. Tactics range from very broad marketing vehicles that reach a large number of potential customers (television and radio) to more focused tactics that may reach potential customers in very specific areas (flyers, billboards) or when they're looking for specific information (online advertising and text ads).

The next sections will explore some of the most popular marketing tactics in depth, discussing the pros and cons of each vehicle and providing specific guidance. They discuss the types of businesses that may find value in each particular topic and give some straight-forward advice about how to leverage these tactics in the real world.

We provide you with a lot of details about the process here. We don't expect that you'll memorize everything in one read through. This book should serve as a resource, not only in helping to determine which tactics are right for you, but also as you go through the process itself. Keep the book around, mark pages, underline things, and generally feel free to use it in whatever way helps you the most.

If you have a particular tactic in mind, feel free to jump directly to that section. You may find as much value in exploring a brand new tactic as you do picking up some new tips on a tactic you've used for years. We also provide links to specific resources on our website.

5

TELEVISION ADVERTISING

Overview

Television advertising can be an expensive endeavor. A national advertiser like General Motors, Procter & Gamble, or Coca-Cola commonly spend hundreds of thousands of dollars to produce a television commercial and then invest tens or even hundreds of millions annually to air it. Large companies or brands will often produce multiple television advertisements to communicate slightly different messages and to avoid "wear-out," an industry term for what happens when customers get tired of a particular advertisement and begin to ignore it.

So, if television advertising is so expensive, why would a small business ever consider it?

The truth is, many companies that invest in TV advertising spend significantly less than the examples presented above. At the much less expensive end of the spectrum, it's possible to produce a television spot using a local production company or freelance director for a few thousand dollars and to air the spot with the local affiliate of a national network for less than $10 per thousand viewers. In a mid-sized city, a specific program may have one hundred thousand viewers, and a thirty-second spot could cost you less than $1,000 to air. This means that a ten-spot contract during that program would cost you less than $10,000, plus the money you spent to produce the spot (not including a few other incidental expenses). Of course, expenses will vary widely depending on your region, the network(s), the show(s) you choose to advertise on, the time of year, and the production company you use. But, the point is, it is possible for a small business to afford to advertise on TV.

If this sounds too inexpensive to be true, bear in mind that we're not talking about airing during a national prime-time program or having the slick, high production value of a Coca-Cola ad. Your marketing effort would be a bit more basic in some respects.

If you want to generate awareness of your company among a very large audience, you'll probably need to spend more than what's described in the example above. But it may all be worth it, and, if done well, your final effort may look pretty polished.

Despite the many other advertising vehicles that have come along, including the Internet, there seems to be something about television advertisements that reinforce the image of your company as not only a reputable business, but a leader in the space. Many customers believe there is something more "legitimate" about a company that they've seen in a television advertisement.

Consider your own experience when grocery shopping. Do you find yourself more likely to buy a nationally advertised brand versus one you've never heard of—even if the products themselves seem very similar?

When Does Television Advertising Make Sense?

Even if your cousin owns a commercial production company and you golf with the general manager of the local television affiliate, television advertising still may not be worth the expense. This is because, in addition to your target customers, you'll be reaching a very large number of people who simply aren't interested in what you have to offer. They may live too far from your business, or they may not be interested for countless other reasons.

The types of businesses that tend to benefit the most from television advertising are:

- businesses centrally located within the viewing area
- businesses with multiple locations spread out within the viewing area
- businesses with delivery to a broad area
- "destination" businesses (businesses that have a unique offering that customers are willing to travel some distance for)
- businesses in a smaller city, where it's easier for residents to travel across the entire area
- businesses that appeal to a very broad segment of customers

TV advertising for relatively small, single-location businesses may not make sense, simply because you'll be wasting money on too many people who aren't very likely to ever purchase from you. As with any marketing vehicle, the key is to spend your money most efficiently by using tactics that reach the largest number of people who are most likely to respond and doing so at the lowest cost per person. Naturally, you also want to communicate the most appealing message you can while you're at it. (Review the Messaging section for more on this.)

Put another way, it makes more sense for a Coca-Cola or Tide laundry detergent to advertise on television. Lots and lots of people in nearly every area, are potential customers for Coke or Tide. It may be less likely that anyone, anywhere will rush to your specific business when there may be viable alternatives closer to them.

If your business meets one of the criteria outlined above, or you've determined for another reason that television advertising is the way to go, read the next sections which discuss the two principal elements (and expense categories) of television advertising: producing the commercial and airing it.

We discuss commercial production first and airing the commercial second because it's a logical flow. However, because purchasing media (air time) may require a longer lead time than making the actual television commercial, you may want to consider purchasing the media first.

Producing a Television Commercial

The Message

The traditional television advertisement is fifteen or thirty seconds long. Obviously, this is not a lot of time to communicate everything you'd like to say about your business—which is why you'll need to choose what you'd like to say carefully. If you've read the Messaging section, you may already have a good sense for the one or two priorities you'd like to communicate.

Some things to bear in mind, in addition to your main message, when considering what to include in a TV commercial:

- A picture is worth a thousand words: Television advertising is a visual medium. When considering what to include in your ad, ask yourself a few questions: Is there anything about your business that customers must see to believe? Is there something about your business that has great visual appeal? Is there anything you can visually demonstrate to a customer that will help seal the deal? If the answer to any of these questions is "yes," then show it—but be decisive in what you show. In addition to including enough time for a customer to absorb the visual, you may have additional things to communicate.

- Improve recall: Television viewing is a relatively passive activity. It's rare that a customer will get up from the couch to make a phone call or write down an address or telephone number. If you're going to share this information with a potential customer, do it in a way that's very easy to remember. Consider showing customers what the outside of your business looks like—or at least show them the sign—so they'll recognize and remember it the next time they drive or walk by. If appropriate, show customers the surrounding area to help cement the location in their minds, or show them a picture of a simple map with your location clearly highlighted. If you include your phone number, repeat it several times and/or use letters rather than numbers so that it's easier to remember (555-MY PLACE).

- Ad approval: Many first-time advertisers don't realize that the media outlet (your local network affiliate) is under no obligation to accept your ad. They may ask for substantiation of any specific claims you make (e.g., "Customers agree our offering is the best in town"). This is to protect them in the event that they are named as a codefendant in a possible lawsuit by a customer group or competitor. Naturally, this is rare, but it does happen.

Certain types of things work particularly well in television advertising—specifically, visual images that do an excellent job of selling a key feature of your business. (Hopefully, this is linked closely to your primary message.) If you choose to invest in television advertising, you'll find some content ideas below.

- Specialty food: Highlight a specialty food, particularly if "seeing is believing." You may consider showing someone eating and enjoying

---

the meal (e.g. enjoying your specialty ice-cream) or the meal itself if it has particular camera appeal (e.g. a juicy steak, a giant burrito, fresh lobster in the tank). Maybe you have a huge buffet full of enticing delights.

- Highlight the restaurant ambiance. Show how enticing the rich, quiet, candlelit décor can be. Show the spectacular view from your roof-top deck. Entice diners with a historical location or building. Highlight the beautiful people who frequent your establishment. Show kids enjoying the family-friendly environment.

- Highlight the chef. You may show the chef in action (e.g. sushi chef preparing a meal or a chef preparing a show-stopping flambé).

- Show them the entertainment. Maybe you have a stage, a DJ, or spectacular artwork. While this shouldn't necessarily be the primary message, you may highlight it as one of several visuals in your commercial.

- Feature an endorsement. A word of support from a recognizable local or national celebrity can serve as a great endorsement. Make sure the person is not particularly polarizing or you risk turning off as many people as you attract. It would also help if something about the person is a good fit with your restaurant. (e.g. a sports star talking about his favorite restaurant by the ballpark).

- Use sound to support your images. Finally, TV enables you to utilize sound to help create the

> mood as well. Carefully chosen music can highlight an ethnic cuisine or serve to reinforce the ambiance.

Selecting and Hiring a Director and Producer

A producer manages all aspects of the commercial production process, including the creative production and business aspects. This is not to be confused with the director, who is principally in charge of the creative aspects of the commercial. Think of the producer as the project manager and the director as the guy yelling at the actors and the camera crew. With smaller production companies, it's not unusual for the producer and director to be the same individual or for both to be employees of the same company.

If required, the producer will hire and manage the director, script writer, director of photography (the person in charge of actually filming the commercial), editor, and actors/actresses, among others. Again, with a small production company, a single person may fill many of these roles. The company itself may consist of only a few people. Regardless of how many people you're dealing with, you should negotiate a flat fee with the producer and allow him or her to manage all aspects of the shoot. The producer should also ensure the final product is in the correct format for the local media outlet.

As with any other vendor selection decision, you'll probably want to do a bit of research, interview a few production resources, and ask for references and samples of their work.

There are several resources you can use to help find a producer:

- Local advertisers: See a TV ad for a local business that you thought was done well? Call the manager/owner and ask for the producer's contact information. While you're at it, and if the manager is willing, you might as well ask for a reference. How did the manager like working with the company?

- The internet: A professional television producer should have a website. This will serve as a great resource, as it will likely contain samples of work for your review. Search the term "video production" or "video advertising agency" plus your city's name for listings of producers in your area. There are also a few good resources that enable you to submit a brief and have several directors create commercials for you on spec. You award the money based on the commercial you like the best and ask the winning director to make changes as appropriate.

- Networks: Local networks will sometimes offer to produce the spot themselves, or they may be willing to refer several local production professionals. Although the network may undercut other producers in the area, it's important to view the spots they've produced and compare them to your other bids. They may or may not deliver the quality standards you demand.

- Media agencies: Media agencies will also be able to provide you with local references or may offer to do the work themselves. This will end up being slightly more expensive than finding a producer on your own, but the agency's expertise may be worth the extra time and money.

- Our site: We provide a few additional resources that may be helpful.

Production Costs and Legal Considerations

You should be aware of several issues when developing a television commercial. A good producer will guide you through the process, but, as with all business deals, you should ask your attorney to evaluate the elements of the production contract as well.

Production costs. A producer should include "fully-loaded" costs in the estimate. These costs will include writing, directing, all production materials, all equipment, site rental fees (if applicable), and any other miscellaneous fees related to production. You don't want to find an incremental line item for hotel expenses for the producer, director, and talent unexpectedly added to your bill at the final hour. The production fee should also include exclusive rights to the final product (though it's typical to permit the producer and/or director to retain a copy of the commercial as part of a personal "reel"). Many times these costs will not include talent and music rights, which might be negotiated separately.

Talent. In the case of a small, regional production, the actors' fees will probably end up being paid as a flat fee. However, there is a chance the producer will use an actor(s) who is associated with a talent union. The cost for most union talent in the U.S. is dictated by the Screen Actors Guild. There are different, defined rates for "principal" actors and "extras," and the definition of what constitutes each can be fairly complex. Also, union talent is typically paid with the understanding that the ad will run for a specific period of time. If you later decide to air your commercial for longer than what was agreed upon, you'll need to renegotiate and pay for the extension. These things probably won't apply if a flat fee is negotiated with nonunion talent. If union talent it used, the producer should help you navigate every step of this process. If you remember nothing else, remember to ask whether your actors are union or not and consider getting some help negotiating and understanding the fine print if they are.

Music. If you have music in your commercial, you'll need to purchase the rights. This may not be particularly expensive and also may be paid as a single flat fee that will cover you for as long as you air the commercial. Of course, if you want a specific song in your spot, you should be prepared to shell out more money, which may or may not be feasible. Whatever the case —even if the producer's sister records a track for use in your commercial at no additional charge—you'll want to make sure you're protected by ensuring the contract includes your right to use the music in the commercial for as long as you choose to air it.

The right to use the commercial elsewhere. You may want to post your commercial to your website or use it in other vehicles aside from traditional television. Even if you don't think this is a possibility at the time you negotiate the contract, consider including all rights for any media vehicle in perpetuity in the contract anyway. With a local producer and local talent, there's a strong possibility that this won't cost you much (if anything), and you'll be covered. When in doubt, simply try to include "universal rights" in the contract, particularly if it costs you nothing.

Steps in the Production Process

The process of producing a television advertisement need not be complicated, but it's helpful to understand all the steps so you know what to expect, how to prepare, and what types of questions to ask a potential producer in the bidding process.

Also, try to have fun. Not everyone gets to be involved in the production of something that will air on television. Embrace your inner Hollywood! But remember that the producer and director are the experts. Be involved enough to get the result you want, but also try not to micromanage the process. Know when to step back and let them work their magic.

1. Know what you want: Decide what type of commercial you'd like to produce and what you'd like to say. Ideally, you'll include this in the form of a creative brief. This will help you select the ideal producer for the type of spot you'd like to create and help you with your negotiations.
2. Select the producer: See the preceding section. At this stage, you should be interviewing, checking references, clearly explaining what you want, and negotiating the fully-loaded costs—as well as agreeing to the proposed incremental cost for talent and music and other incidentals, if applicable.
3. Pre-production: Once the producer understands what you're looking for, his or her team goes to work

selecting the appropriate talent, site, props, and all other elements that go into production. You'll then hold a meeting (called the pre-production meeting or "pre-pro") to review all proposed elements to ensure you are aligned before production begins. Make sure you understand everything and can visualize the final product at this stage, as going back and making changes later can add significant cost and valuable time to the production. You want it done right the first time.

4. Production: The actual shoot can often take a full day. The director will carefully set up each scene and capture multiple takes (sometimes many more than you'd expect for a single thirty-second spot). This will ensure there's plenty of material to work with at the editing stage in case one or more shots are not working well with the finished product. This stage may also include a separate session in a recording studio to record a voiceover or other sound elements.

5. Post-production/editing. This is when the footage is edited into that perfect fifteen or thirty-second spot, music is added, sound and light levels are adjusted, etc. The director or producer should consult with you during this process to ensure you like how the piece is coming together.

6. Shipping: When you've agreed on the final product, the producer should ensure the video file is in the correct format and ship the final copy (or copies) to the stations or networks that will air your spot. Be sure to ask the producer about storing the "master," and make sure you get your own copy for future use. Preferably, get a digital copy so you can add it to your website.

Airing a Television Commercial

In airing the commercial, you'll need to determine who your target audience is (see the Targeting section) and match this with the various television networks and shows in your area. To determine this, you'll need to contact the advertising sales departments of your local television stations (typically local affiliates of national networks like ABC, NBC, etc.) and ask them for local advertising rates and for information about the viewers of each program on their network.

This info will typically be demographic (age, income) but may include some psychographic information (attitudes, behaviors). Ten thousand viewers of a reality show are often very different people than ten thousand viewers of the evening news. Naturally, your decisions depend on which viewer is more likely to become a customer of your business.

Alternately, you can simply tell them who you're trying to reach and ask them what the best program might be to help you do so. The downside of this is that the network is likely to encourage you to advertise on a program which is looking for sponsors and which may or may not be the best choice for you.

Ad Rates

Advertising rates depend primarily on one factor: the number of viewers who tune in to the television program you'd like to advertise on. (Although, time of year and demand for advertising space will also be factors.) A show's popularity is measured by a company called Nielsen and is expressed in terms of ratings points/share. The programs are often rated on both the national and local levels. (Naturally, you'll be most interested in the local ratings). If there are three million television viewing households in your city or network area, and a specific program has a "two share" according to Nielsen, this means that program is watched by two percent, or sixty thousand households. While the validity of this measurement system is debated, the reality is, it's still the standard by which "reach" is measured and advertising rates are set.

A typical thirty-minute television show block of time will be filled with twenty-two minutes of actual programming (the show) and the remaining eight minutes is allocated to advertising, typically in thirty-second blocks. If those spots are nearly full, your rate goes up. If the spots are not filled, you might get a bargain. For this reason, the published rates per point are merely a starting point and don't necessarily reflect current market conditions. In this respect, they're a bit like the MSRP on a new car.

Timeframe

It's not uncommon for all the commercial slots for a popular program to be booked well in advance. For that reason, you should discuss purchasing media in advance of when you'd actually like to air it—usually as much as a quarter (three months) in advance. This will help ensure you get the placement you want and can also help your negotiating position. You also have the option of purchasing remnant (unsold) inventory during shows that are currently airing. This is sometimes also called "spot" or "scatter" inventory. Often, these spots are filled with teasers for the network's other programs or by nonprofit advertising, so a good way to judge how much advertising is still available during a program is to watch the program yourself, keeping an eye out for these types of ads.

Media Placement Agencies

There are agencies that can help you navigate the process of airing your television spot. These agencies typically charge a percentage of what you'll end up paying for advertising (their commission) but may also be willing to work on a flat-fee basis. They make their money by negotiating discounts to advertising rates and charging you the "standard rate" or something in between, essentially splitting the savings. For this reason, even though it may seem as if you have to pay yet another agency, you may actually save yourself money.

Media agencies may be very helpful in determining which networks and programs best meet your needs, in negotiating the process, and in assisting you and your producer in shipping the actual advertisement. They may also be able to help you measure the success of your advertising and determine an airing schedule that will maximize your advertising dollars by generating the most "views" for the least amount of money. Finally, they'll help you by saving quite a bit of your own time in the process.

But, as with any agency, a media placement agency is in business to make money. The best policy is to treat hiring a media agency as you would any other contractor decision: bid your business out to more than one agency and ask for references. All things considered, you're probably a bit better off getting the help—especially if you're new to the TV advertising world. You can find an agency by searching online for "media buying agency."

It's worth noting a few additional things about these types of agencies:

- Local versus national: Unlike a video producer, you are not necessarily better off with a local media buyer. Media may be bought from any location.

- Big versus small: You may be tempted to use a smaller organization, assuming a national media agency will be more expensive or treat your local business as a nuisance rather than a potential revenue stream. While it's true that big advertisers bring in more money for a media agency, your business will not require the full resources that a national advertiser demands and may therefore be worthy of a discount. As with anything else, if you bid the business, you may be surprised by the results.

- Multipurpose: Many agencies today wear multiple hats to better serve their advertising partners and to capitalize on more of the advertising dollars being spent. It's very likely that any or all of the media placement firms you work with will also offer video production services. And they most certainly will be able to purchase other forms of media for you, including print, radio, and online. For this reason, it may be to your advantage to consult with a media agency prior to determining which advertising vehicle you'd like to use.

A Note on DRTV

You may have heard of DRTV (direct response television). If you haven't, you've probably seen an infomercial—typically a longer-format half-hour show designed to sell a product or service. Infomercials are a sub-segment of DRTV. In a broader sense, DRTV simply refers to any television commercial that seeks to generate a "direct response," which can mean encouraging a customer to visit a website or call a phone number. Although a half-hour program format is probably not right for your business (unless you offer something that's fairly complex), your commercial may be considered a DRTV spot, particularly if you are trying to encourage customers to take a specific action. This can be important, because networks are sometimes willing to offer discounts for DRTV advertisements. It's worth asking about this policy when you contact your local affiliate or discuss your strategy with a media agency.

Television Summary

- Television advertising is best for large regional businesses that cover a broad area. Smaller regional businesses may want to consider other media.
- Television is a visual medium. When developing an ad, use visuals to your advantage by showing things that customers need to see.
- A local production company will typically handle all key aspects of the shoot, including production, talent, and

editing. Bid your business, consider references, and have an attorney review the contract.

- Leave yourself enough time. The process of creating a television ad can take several months from start to final air date—especially your first time.

- Local affiliates of national television stations will negotiate your ad rates with you directly, or you may hire a media agency to negotiate on your behalf.

6

RADIO ADVERTISING

Overview

It comes as a surprise to many first-time radio advertisers that radio can be as expensive as television. Radio stations can demand these types of prices because they typically cover the entire city and may reach as many customers as a local television station can—particularly during drive time or rush hour. Typically, radio stations get the most listeners during morning and evening commutes. However, rates can vary dramatically, depending on the station and time of day.

As with all types of advertising, radio has pros and cons.

Cons: The same caveats apply to radio advertising as local television advertising. Radio advertising may not be worth the expense for many local advertisers because you'll be reaching a large number of people who are unlikely to become your customers. They may live too far from your business location, or there may be a convenient and familiar substitute close by. If your service area is smaller than the entire radio listening area, then you'll always be wasting a bit of money on people who will never become customers.

Which types of businesses find radio advertising ideal? The same types of businesses will benefit from radio advertising that benefit from television:

- businesses centrally located within the listening area
- businesses with multiple locations spread out within the listening area
- businesses with delivery to a broad area
- "destination" businesses (businesses that have a unique offering that customers are willing to travel some distance for)
- businesses in a smaller city, where it's easier for residents to travel across the entire area

Pros: Now a few of the benefits. Radio advertising does have some important advantages over other traditional forms of advertising:

- Fast turnaround: A radio advertisement can be produced relatively quickly—and may not need to be produced at all (you can pay for a DJ to promote your product online with little more than a script or talking points). Air time can often be purchased with relatively fast turnaround times as well, particularly outside of drive time. So, if you are interested in getting a message out quickly, you should consider radio.

- Drive time: Because many customers are in their cars, driving home during prime evening commute hours, there's a better possibility that you can get someone to drive to your place of business that evening—especially if you instill a sense of immediacy (e.g. advertise a special that takes place today or this week only). Contrast this with the more passive viewing experience TV offers.

- Low cost for multiple spots: If you're developing a script and paying for studio time and a voiceover artist, it's relatively inexpensive—potentially very inexpensive—to create an additional one, two, or more spots while you're at it. (If you're paying a DJ to read a script, it may actually be slightly more expensive, as you'll typically pay per script/read.) Use this opportunity to highlight monthly specials, special events, or whatever is timely.

Creating the Radio Spot

The Message

The traditional radio advertisement is thirty seconds long. This is not a lot of time to communicate everything you'd like to say about your business, which is why you'll need to choose exactly what you say carefully. If you've read the section on messaging, you may already have a good sense for the one or two priorities you'd like to communicate.

Some things to bear in mind in addition to your main message when considering what to include in a radio commercial:

- Time of day: If you've purchased time during an evening commute, you'll want to take advantage of the opportunity to convince the customer to call or stop by your place of business tonight (if applicable). Consider what you might say to your potential customer if you were sitting in the car seat beside him or her (in a thirty-second conversation, of course). Why should they go? Where are you located? What's your phone number? (They will likely have a cell phone with them.) Anything special going on right now?

- Ad approval: As with television, many first-time advertisers don't realize that the media outlet (your local radio station) is under no obligation to accept your ad. They may ask for substantiation of any specific claims you make (e.g., our service was voted the best in town). This is to protect them in the event that they are named as a codefendant in a claim brought by a customer group, competitor, etc.

Finally, a few notes about the script itself: Many small business owners opt to write their own scripts. This will save you some money, but bear in mind that radio can be a tricky medium. The script will not only need to convey important and compelling information about your business, but it should do so in an engaging and entertaining way. There are lots of things competing for the attention of the average radio listener—not the least of which may be the other drivers during a morning or evening commute.

If you do decide to write your own script, spend some time closely listening to a few radio ads to pick up tips about things you think are effective and engaging, as well as what doesn't work. Finally, read the script out loud a few times to ensure it fits comfortably within the thirty seconds allotted without rushing.

If you decide to search for a scriptwriter, try some local agencies or ask a production studio for suggestions.

Option 1: Produce Your Spot

The production and editing of your radio spot can normally be done in a recording studio. To find studios in your area, simply search online for "recording studio (city name)" or "radio commercial production (city name)." Most studios have all the equipment and staff required to edit and finish your spot in house—so you'll walk out of the studio with your finished radio spot in hand. Studios typically charge an hourly rate, which may or may not include editing and final production of the spot. As with any contract, ensure you understand what is and is not included.

Talent: You may decide to act as your own voiceover talent by speaking the lines of the script yourself. There may be several good reasons for doing this, including saving money or implying to the listener that you care enough about your own business to deliver a promise personally. Consider carefully before you do this, however. Voiceover artists collect fees for a reason. Often, their voices are interesting and engaging and are therefore very effective at capturing the listener's attention for that crucial thirty seconds that the ad has to deliver a message. They are also often very good at ensuring the most important information carries extra emphasis without sounding artificial. If you do decide to use talent, find it by using a local talent/casting agency. There are several online resources for information here as well.

If you use professional talent, you'll often end up being subject to a union-defined pay scale. These pay scales can be difficult to understand and negotiate, so ensure that you discuss the details with the agent and understand the terms and restrictions. Often, the fee you pay will cover a certain period of time and number of airings. If you reuse the commercial or run it for longer than the negotiated period, you will need to renegotiate the fee with the agency for the additional time.

Music: Music often helps add some engagingness to your radio commercial. (But be careful. It can also be distracting.) If you'd like music in your ad, you'll typically need to pay the copyright owner for its use. Like talent, you'll typically pay the owner of the song for a specified use and period of time. The cost of music varies widely. As you might expect, the cost to use a popular song in your advertising will be very expensive, usually prohibitively so. However, there are significantly less expensive music sources you can use, including paying someone to create a custom piece of music specifically for your commercial. Contrary to what you may think, this may be very inexpensive. Often, the recording studio can recommend someone or may have a musician on staff who can add simple background music to your spot. Music can be a bit like paint on the walls—you might not immediately notice the color, but the paint can add (or subtract) measurably from the overall effect, often in a very subtle but important way.

Before you leave the studio, ensure you're happy with the final result—particularly the voiceover. You don't want to pay for another full session or waste your own time. Ensure the final spot fits within the thirty-second window required by the radio station. (It doesn't hurt to be a second under to allow for transition time.) Listen to the entire commercial again and ensure you're happy with the "levels." This means listening to the individual audio elements of the spot, including each voiceover (if there is more than one), the music, and any sound effects. Make sure one particular sound element doesn't overwhelm another. This is exactly the work that studios are experts at. If you have questions or concerns, have them explain to you what they've done.

Option 2: Pay a Local DJ(s) to Read Your Script on Air

Rather than recording a custom spot at a studio, you can simply pay a DJ at a local radio station to read the script. (You'll also need to pay for the air time as if this were any other commercial.) There are some important pros and cons to consider here.

Potential upsides include:

• Endorsement: Local DJs often have devoted fans who will listen when that DJ offers advice. Many advertisers believe a DJ read provides an implied—or often overt—endorsement of the product or service being advertised.

- Engaging: While many listeners tune out traditional advertising, either subconsciously or literally (by changing the station), those same listeners may be less likely to tune out a "commercial" being delivered by the DJ.

Potential downsides include:

- Non-Scalable: A spot read by a DJ of one station cannot be used on another station, and it often can't be used on the same station after the term of the contract expires. Even if it could be used on another station, the value and recognition that comes with a particular DJ would be lost. If you decide that a single, specific radio station is the ideal fit for your target, this may not be an issue.

- Ad lib: This can be a positive or a negative, depending on how it goes. The DJ will occasionally go off script and make his or her own observations about your business. You may be pleased with the result, but there's also a chance you may not be. Even the most well intentioned comment may not be in line with the image you're trying to create.

As mentioned, radio advertisements are a visual medium. Use this to your advantage by determining what sounds and which people can have the greatest impact.

- Choose your spokesperson carefully:
  - As mentioned earlier, you may choose to have a local celebrity or radio personality highlight the benefits of your restaurant. If you can work with the celebrity to get

a more personal sounding endorsement, this is ideal. Have they been to the restaurant? If not, do they know someone who has? Is there an item on your menu that they typically enjoy and might rave about? Can you include them in an upcoming event? If so, have them talk about it!

o You might choose to talk about the restaurant yourself. If so, this is an endorsement of sorts. It says that the owner takes personal pride in the restaurant and wants to talk about what sets it apart from the competition.

o You may also want your chef to talk about the food and the care he or she puts into its selection and preparation. Similarly, you could have a sommelier talk about the wine selection or a bartender talk about the terrific beer selection.

o If service is important, you may want to feature someone who plays the part of a friendly waiter/waitress and who talks about the enjoyable atmosphere.

o Finally, you could also consider featuring a "diner" or several customers who discuss how much they enjoy the restaurant, food, and the atmosphere or other benefit you consider important and differentiating. "Overhearing" people discuss your restaurant can often generate a powerful word-of-mouth effect, even though the listener knows these are actors and actresses.

- <u>Ethnic Cues</u>: Specific ethnic food may become even more enticing if you replicate the sounds, music, or ambiance of the ethnicity you are trying to capture. You may also feature a spokesperson with a regional accent. But be cautious about overdoing it. You do not want to come off as a caricature of the culture. Let the effect add to the atmosphere without distracting from your main message.

- <u>Humor</u>: Humor can work well in radio but humor is often difficult to get right. People have very different ideas about what is considered funny and something you believe is funny may even offend potential customers. If humor is important to the spot, consider hiring a writer. If you go it alone, try a "less is more" approach. Sometimes simply being light-hearted can be enough.

Airing the Radio Spot

In airing the commercial, you'll need to determine who your target audience is (refer to the Targeting section) and match this with the various radio stations in your area. To do this, you'll need to contact the advertising sales departments of your local radio stations and ask them for advertising rates and information about programs' listeners, which may be both demographic (age, income) and psychographic (attitudes, behaviors). Radio is a much more local medium than television, and sales are often conducted at the local level. A few large national radio media properties exist—perhaps the best known is Clear Channel Communications, headquartered in San Antonio, which operates more than 1,200 radio stations. But normally even local Clear Channel affiliates are empowered to negotiate advertising contracts with local advertisers. Another national property, Sirius/XM satellite radio, is typically ad free but does sell advertising on some stations.

Ad Rates

Similar to television, radio advertising rates depend primarily on one core factor: the number of listeners who tune in to the radio station during the time you'd like to advertise. (Although, time of year and demand for advertising space will also be factors.) This popularity is measured by a company called Arbitron and is expressed in terms of ratings points/share. These ratings can be both national and local. If there are three million households in your city or network area, and a specific program has a two share, that program reaches sixty thousand households. While the validity of this measurement system is debated, the reality is, it's still the standard by which "reach" is measured and advertising rates are set.

Timeframe

While many national and local advertisers purchase radio spots, a radio program often will have additional space available, many times on very short notice. For this reason, radio is a good vehicle to use to get a message out to potential customers quickly and broadly.

Media Placement Agencies

There are agencies that will help you navigate the process of airing your radio spot. These agencies typically charge a percentage of the advertising expense but may also be willing to work on a flat-fee basis. They make their money by negotiating discounts to advertising rates and charging you the "standard rate" or a slightly discounted rate. Typically, the agencies that help you purchase radio spots will be the same agencies that can help you purchase TV spots. See the Television section for advice in dealing with them.

Media agencies may be very helpful in determining which stations and times best meet your needs, in helping you measure the success of your advertising, in determining an airing schedule that will maximize your advertising dollars by generating the most "exposures" for the least amount of money, and by saving you quite a bit of your own time in the process. But, like any agency, a media placement agency is in business to make money. The best policy is to treat hiring a media agency as you would any other contractor decision: bid your business out to at least three agencies and ask for references. All things considered, you're probably a bit better off getting the help—especially if you're new to the radio advertising world.

You can find an agency by searching online for "media buying agency." It's worth noting a few additional things about these types of agencies.

- Local versus national: You are not necessarily better off with a local media buyer. Media may be bought from any location.

- Big versus small: You may be tempted to use a smaller organization, assuming a national media agency will be more expensive or treat your local business as a nuisance rather than a potential revenue stream. While it's true that national accounts bring in more money, you typically will not require the full resources that a national advertiser demands. As with anything else, if you bid the business, you may be surprised by the results.

- Multipurpose: Many agencies today wear multiple hats to better serve their advertising partners and to capitalize on more of the advertising dollars being spent. It's possible that any or all of the media placement firms you work with will also offer studio recording services. And they will certainly be able to purchase most other forms of media for you, including print, TV, and online. For this reason, it may be to your advantage to consult with a media agency prior to determining which advertising vehicle you'd like to use.

Other Radio Opportunities

Besides the traditional radio commercial, there are several other opportunities to generate awareness for your business that a radio station may provide:

- Live feed/remote feed: Most local radio stations will charge you a flat fee to broadcast from your location. Typically, this incorporates a full package of services, including regular live DJ announcements about your business, a radio van and promotional signs at your location, free giveaways and contests, live interviews with you and/or members of your staff, and sometimes even on-the-spot customer testimonials. Many times, small business owners will pay for these services to announce an opening or a particularly large special event.

- News/traffic/weather sponsorship: You can pay a radio station for exclusive sponsorship of a particular news segment. Typically, the sponsor is mentioned immediately before or after each segment, which may air as often as every ten minutes during peak drive times. Messaging is typically very brief, consisting of your business name and maybe a brief sales line. In this case, it's particularly important to clearly understand your business's most important and compelling communication element.

- Giveaways: Most radio stations regularly feature contests, call-ins, surveys, and a variety of tools to generate listener engagement and interaction. Typically, they'll include prizes or giveaways to callers. You can send the local radio station certificates for discounts or other merchandise to use for these giveaways. If the station includes your giveaway in a "prize pack," there's no guarantee you'll get a specific mention—but, the higher the value, the better the chance of a mention. It may be worth the expense to offer the radio station a particularly large prize in exchange for the air time and recognition you'll get. A radio station may make several mentions of a prize pack that includes something valuable or something particularly unique.

Radio Summary

- Radio advertising is best for large regional businesses that cover a broad area. Smaller regional businesses may want to consider other media.
- Radio is "theater of the mind," with no images to help sell your business. When developing an ad, ensure it is entertaining and engaging and that it communicates key calls to action (like telephone numbers) multiple times.
- A production studio will typically handle all key aspects of the recording session, including talent and editing. Bid your business, consider references, and have an attorney review the contract.

- Consider having a professional who knows what audiences respond to write your script for you.

- Radio stations will negotiate your ad rates with you directly, or you may hire a media agency to negotiate on your behalf.

- There are several radio-related options for you to consider, including traditional produced spots; live or recorded DJ reads; live remote feeds on location; news, traffic, or weather sponsorships; and radio giveaways.

7

PRINT ADVERTISING

Overview

Print covers a broad range of vehicles and may be defined differently by different people. We define "print" as any printed material designed to reach an audience with the intention of educating or entertaining—not something with the sole purpose of advertising. This would include magazines, newspapers, and newsletters. In contrast to this, an example of material that serves mainly as an advertising vehicle would be a coupon mailer.

Although similar in some respects, we consider billboard and online communications different enough from print that we discuss them in their own sections. Another related vehicle, public relations, which often enables a business to get mentioned in printed articles, is also discussed in a separate section.

Some of the most common print vehicles are discussed below, but this is by no means an exhaustive list. There may be other interesting and innovative print vehicles in your area. Regardless of vehicle type, the principles of advertising in these vehicles are similar.

Print vehicles differ from television and radio in that print publications often cater to specific interests. Even generalist publications (like local newspapers or citywide magazines) tend to have specific sections or special issues dedicated to areas of specific interest. Often, it's within these specific interest areas that your advertising will have the greatest impact.

The same caveats apply to print advertising as those that apply to local television and radio advertising: print advertising may not be worth the expense if your business is concentrated in an area that's smaller than the print circulation. You'll likely be reaching a large number of people who are unlikely to become your customers. They may live too far from your place of business or may have familiar businesses closer to them.

Many cities have special-interest print publications that may specifically appeal to your customer base. These customers may be willing to go a bit out of their way to visit your business if it seems worthwhile.

Creating a Print Advertisement

While not as complex a process as producing a television commercial, you'll still probably want to hire an expert (a print production house or agency) to help you produce your print ad—particularly if you plan to include visuals such as a picture, sketch, or logo. Other elements a professional will work with are the layout of the commercial and ensuring the commercial is in a specific format and meets all of the media provider's other requirements, including digital and color format, ad size, and bleed (the extra space outside the actual ad to allow for very slight variations in size).

There are several resources you can use to find a local graphic artist, print producer, or agency:

- Local advertisers: See an ad for a local business in a publication that you thought was well done? Call the manager/owner and ask for the contact information of the print producer or agency. While you're at it, ask the manager what he or she thought of the artist/producer/agency.
- The internet: Most artists and agencies will have a website, which will likely contain samples of their work. Search the terms "graphic artist (your city)," "print advertising production (your city)," or "print advertising agency (your city)" for listings of producers in your area.
- Print publications: Many print publications will be willing to refer a local graphic professional to you. They may even be willing to produce the ad themselves, though you'll want to compare quality and price to other professionals in a bid process.
- Media agency: Media agencies will also be able to provide you with local references or may offer to do the work themselves. Just as with print publications, you'll want to obtain a bid from someone else to compare.

Customers who are paging through a magazine or

newspaper are doing so for the content, not the ads. Consider your own reading habits. A reader will typically see an ad very briefly as he or she flips the page. As the advertiser, you have seconds to register a message with the customer. You'll want this message to be engaging so that they're willing to learn more. Think of a print advertisement as needing to do two separate jobs:

1. Capture the reader's attention: Often this can be done with compelling visuals, i.e., a picture of your company's most compelling visual feature. Whatever visual you select, it should also say something important about the best reason to visit your business. The visual doesn't need to be a photograph. Perhaps a cartoon or another graphical element can better convey what you want to say in a compelling way.

2. Provide extra information: Once you've hooked the potential customer with your visual, you'll also want to provide the most relevant information the customer needs to make the decision to visit or call. Select the most important additional elements that you need to tell customers (main message plus location, specific offerings, hours, other selling features). You don't have room for a book here, so be sure you select the must-have information and that it doesn't distract from the primary benefit—your key selling feature.

> Because people will typically see your ad quickly, determine what ONE image will represent your restaurant the best and ensure it looks good! Examples of things that you might want to show in a print advertisement:

- Food: People love pictures of food. For proof, look at any social media or review site. However, people typically take pictures only of food they consider unusual or exceptionally well prepared. Choose one or two dishes that you consider a hallmark of your restaurant and ensure they look very well prepared and mouth-watering. Some photographers specialize in food and can ensure that lighting, presentation, and even moisture effects make your food look absolutely mouth-watering on the page. If you pride yourself on fresh ingredients, you may decide to show the ingredients rather than the finished product, or some point in the food preparation process. In this case, it may be even more important to ensure that the ingredients look beautiful and appetizing. Consider getting the help of a professional photographer!

- Atmosphere: Along with food, atmosphere is also one of the key visual experiences that people enjoy about restaurants. For diners focused on a certain ambiance, this is important. And while you want to ensure your establishment looks great in the photo, do not misrepresent the atmosphere. If it's family-friendly, show a family having a great time. This may turn off some diners but will appeal to the ones best suited to your restaurant and those most likely to refer you to like-minded customers. The following are a few specific ideas for how to depict your restaurant character:

- Intimate: You can depict an intimate environment with muted, darker tones, a fireplace, warm candlelight, a table for two, a unique and private table setting(s).
- Social: Groups of people (that best represent your target audience) talking, laughing and generally enjoying themselves, games, if appropriate.
- Family Friendly: Showing a family enjoying themselves with friendly, attentive, and non-judgmental staff may be even more important to a stressed parent than showing the actual food your restaurant serves. This is providing, of course, that the children appear to be enjoying the meal and the environment.

Legal note: Print advertisements may include copyrighted elements and may include people. Both require that you own the rights to use the image in question. Ensure that the fee you're paying your graphic professional includes rights to these elements—and get documentation of it. Ideally, rights should include all uses in perpetuity (which will allow you to use the print spot anywhere, any time at your discretion, including online, in flyers, in sales materials, on location, etc.). If your rights extend only through a specific time period, make sure you understand this as well.

When in doubt, consult your attorney.

Advertising Rates

Most publications have standard advertising rates, typically published on a rate card. These "published rates" represent the highest cost you'll have to pay. It's often possible to negotiate down, particularly with the help of a media agency. It also helps if you're a more frequent advertiser, if you're buying as part of a trade group, or perhaps even if you're a first-time advertiser who is "testing" the vehicle with the potential of advertising more.

Rate cards will typically include the following:

- Specific publication: This is important when a media property produces multiple magazines, newspapers, etc. The rate may cover one or multiple publications.

- Demographics: details about the readership, including age, sex, income, and other key factors that help you determine the fit with your target audience.

- Duration/number of spots: Buying four spots in a weekly publication is not necessarily better than one spot in a monthly publication. The same number of readers may see both (although the number of times a customer sees an ad can be helpful).

- Size: Ads may range in size from a full page to a relatively small portion of a page, to a few text lines (more typical of newspapers or a phone book).

- Position: Rates will be higher for advertisements that appear in a prominent position (e.g., front or back cover).

- Other: There are many other factors that determine rate, depending on the publication. A phone book may charge you to feature your listing in bold type. Other options may exist that are specific to that publication.

Types of Publications

Magazines

Advertising in a magazine can be a bit more complex and potentially more expensive than other print advertising forms, simply because you'll need to create a nice-looking color ad.

Local publications are not your only option here—many national publications are able to serve local advertisers by inserting their ads only in copies distributed locally. (Not all publishers have this capability, however.) If you find a national magazine that you believe is a perfect fit for you, it's worth calling the publication to ask. You can typically find the contact information for any magazine or periodical on or near the first page of the issue's table of contents. If the advertising sales department is not listed specifically, call the general number and ask for the correct department.

The type of magazine that works best for you will depend on your business and your target audience.

Examples of magazines that might be a good fit for a restaurant:
• Food publications: At the risk of stating the obvious, these types of customers are more likely to go out of their way to visit a

> promising restaurant. It's a good idea to include an enticing photo of an entrée.
>
> - Wine or beer enthusiast publications: Same as above. Your ad should focus on wine or beer selection or bar ambiance and fun.
> - Local magazines that include "what to do" sections: Cater to people who are looking to travel outside their immediate areas or break their typical routines. Focus on what's unique about your restaurant.

Newspapers

Although newspapers are not doing as well as they once were due to increased competition from online news sites, they are still an important source of information to many customers and still serve as a very relevant source of local information.

Particularly important to many businesses will be the sections that focus on local customer information. Names for these sections vary but might include "Living," "Lifestyle," "Metro," "Communities," and sometimes "Business." These are the areas of the paper that people visit for specific local information that helps guide their purchase decisions. Therefore, your advertisement will reach customers when they're in a relevant frame of mind.

The process of creating a newspaper ad is similar to the magazine process described above, but there are important differences. Many newspapers have moved to color, but not all have, and the ones that have color might not have it in all sections. There may be an extra charge for a color ad. If you'll be advertising in black and white, you should realize that not all pictures are compelling in this format. Be sure to consider several different options, including graphics or a more basic visual. And, naturally, be sure to view your graphics in a format as similar to the final newspaper format as you can before agreeing to release the ad.

Also important is the classifieds section, which may include a discount or coupon section. This area of the paper is a "direct response" section. Potential customers who visit this section are actively seeking information. Many small businesses choose not to advertise here because the section is viewed as a customer-to-customer space—something akin to eBay. Consider, however, that the classifieds may give you an opportunity to reach potential customers with an interesting offer when they're most likely to write the information down or clip the offer and keep it. The key to a good classified ad is to make a compelling offer (perhaps even an unusual one that grabs the customer's attention) and provide enough information to allow him or her to take advantage of the offer (an address, phone number, or internet address). Also, because the classifieds are not overly expensive, it's possible to experiment with several different types of offers to see which drives the best response.

Not all offers must be discounts, but a discount is still compelling to many customers. A discount tells customers they must act now. These offers are best viewed as a means of driving trial (i.e., compelling someone who has never tried your business to visit or call). Other types of offers can also create a sense of urgency or exclusivity.

Some potentially compelling offers to include in an advertisement:

- Free appetizer or dessert (for parties or checks of a predetermined size)
- Free or discounted admission to an event for the first X reservations
- An opportunity to sample a new or limited-time food entrée
- An opportunity to enter a drawing for a prize
- Exclusive access to a pre-event activity

Phone Books

The internet has almost replaced the traditional Yellow Pages as a resource for local business listings. However, depending on your target audience demographic, you may not want to ignore this vehicle completely. Phone books haven't entirely disappeared and are still in use, particularly among more mature, conservative individuals who may not be entirely comfortable with the internet, as well as lower income individuals who don't have internet access. If your business serves either of these demographics in particular, spreading the word via the Yellow Pages may be a viable opportunity for you.

One of the key benefits of a phone book is its relative permanence. Because phone books are typically released annually, a single advertisement will sit in a customer's home for at least that period of time. Another key benefit is relevance. Your advertisement will appear in the most pertinent section of the phone book, so a customer sees it while searching for relevant listings.

Tactics for advertising in the Yellow Pages range from simply adding boldface to your business's existing listing to make it stand out to creating a separate ad (up to a full page) that can appear close to your listing. You'll need to create this type of advertisement as you would when advertising in a newspaper or magazine.

Rates, especially today, are usually fairly reasonable for this vehicle, but before you jump at the opportunity, consider the relevance of the target demographic.

The Yellow Pages/business listings may also be found online. Online listings may show the location of your business and may provide links to your website, promotional videos, advertisements, etc. More on how to advertise online can be found in the online tactical section of this book.

Other Print Opportunities

There may be many other creative print opportunities in your area that you can take advantage of, particularly if you already have a print advertisement (or several) created in your marketing toolkit.

- Local resident newsletters: Perhaps a local apartment, condo, or housing association has a newsletter that would consider carrying an ad or featuring some kind of discount that the association is able to position as an exclusive opportunity for its members.
- Special-interest publications: Many local areas have special-interest magazines devoted to things that may lend themselves well to your business advertisement.

- Club newsletters: Most local clubs have some type of publication that gets released to members. Find the clubs that are most closely aligned with your target audience and ask about opportunities.

Print Summary

- Print vehicles include magazines, newspapers, phone books, newsletters, or other special-interest publications.
- Print often enables you to target a customer more directly than other "traditional" vehicles like radio or TV.
- You'll be able to target people in the appropriate frame of mind if you carefully choose a publication and a section within that publication based on its relevance to your business.

8

WEBSITE

Overview

Every business should have a website. If you have the goal of attracting new customers, then a website is absolutely mandatory.

In today's world, a company website is a significant source of information that customers look to when researching a business. This is true even if the customer has learned about your business through other means. A customer may see an ad for your business or hear about your business through a friend and want to learn more. They may have a question about something simple like location, hours, or a phone number. Or they may be searching for other details about your business that are not available anywhere else. This is why you need a website.

Website Communication Objectives

The primary objective of your website should be to provide enough information to compel a potential customer to call or visit. It may have the further objective of encouraging a potential customer to purchase something online (a product, gift certificate, etc.).

Unlike a traditional advertisement, in which there is limited time or space to convey a message, a website enables you to provide nearly limitless information about your business. But this doesn't mean a potential customer will find all of it particularly compelling. Often, they'll be seeking something very specific. To avoid making the experience a frustrating one, ensure that the site is simple to navigate and that vital information is easy to find. If you're unclear of what constitutes "vital" information, ask a few of your existing customers or consider the type of information that you yourself search for when researching a business online.

Occasionally, a business owner will become so involved in creating a spectacular website with flash video and wonderful ambiance that the must-have information is buried or never even makes it to the site. The last thing you want is a beautiful site that frustrates a potential customer who is simply trying to find out whether your business is open on Sunday.

Perhaps you believe that if you hold back some of this information, the potential customer may be compelled to call you directly, providing you with the opportunity to close them on the next stage (a visit or a sale.) While this may be true for some customers, others will simply move on to a competitor's site that provides the information they're looking for. Also, you may not be able to guarantee that the person answering the phone can indeed close the potential customer, particularly when that customer may have visited in person had the information been available.

This "must-have" information should be clearly and easily accessible on a restaurant's website:

- Location and contact information: directions are nice as well—in today's world, there's no good excuse for not providing a map or a link to a mapping service like Google Maps.

- Hours and days of operation: if hours change frequently, mention this and include a number to call with an outgoing message that gives the daily/weekly hours of operation.

- Cuisine type: the general category that best describes your menu, even if your menu is a fusion of several types.

- Menu: believe it or not, some restaurants still leave this vital piece of information off their website despite the fact that this is the primary reason customers come in the door. There may be logistical reasons for this, for example, the menu changes too frequently to be reasonably updated. If this is the case, consider including representative offerings or describing the type of food you serve. You don't need to include prices on the menu if this is a concern for you, but bear in mind that some customers will make dining decisions based in part on how reasonable

---

> your prices are. If they cannot readily find this information, they may choose another option that does provide it.
> - Meals served: breakfast, brunch, lunch, dinner, etc.
> - Services offered: catering, delivery, valet, special handicap accessibility features, etc.
> - Specials: happy hours, food specials, senior specials, children's specials, etc.

Your Online Sales Pitch

As with any other advertising vehicle, you should develop your website with your core message in mind. Your site should provide information that supports your key point of differentiation, which is also your primary sales pitch. In addition to the vital information highlighted above, this core messaging information should be easy to find. This doesn't necessarily mean the information resides on the home page. It simply means your site is easy to navigate and has a natural flow that customers find easy and even enjoyable to engage with.

> Beyond the basics outlined above, a website is particularly good at providing detailed information and selling through the use of compelling graphics and moving images. Consider including the following when developing your website:
> - Pictures: Share the ambiance that you believe captures the restaurant's special feel.
> - Links: Link to other sites of relevance to your

establishment. This could be articles or information about specific foods or beverages you offer, links to entertainment such as a band that often plays at your restaurant, or links to news articles about your restaurant.

- Customer testimonials: Enable customers to post their own review on your website or write them yourself by pulling from comments made on comment cards or solicited from your loyal diners. (Never make them up. Many people can spot a false customer review and you certainly don't want word of this to spread.) Ensure you obtain permission. This can be done simply by including a note on the website or physical comment card that states that comments or reviews become the permission of the restaurant and may be used for advertising purposes.

- Articles: Rather than providing a link to the website of a local news outlet or other source that has reviewed your restaurant, you may simply scan and post or reprint the content on your own site. This will often require permission as well. Typically, obtaining this permission is as simple as calling the publication or sending them an email asking to post the content to your site. Publications will typically allow this and often appreciate the additional publicity themselves.

- History: If relevant, you may provide diners with the history of your restaurant, the owners,

> the building itself, or the area. Is the owner originally from Italy (and therefore could be claimed to better understand traditional Italian cuisine?) Is the owner locally or even nationally famous? Is there something particularly notable about your facility that may spark interest and conversation? Did it serve as a speakeasy during prohibition? Has it hosted some famous patrons? Do some people believe it's haunted?

What Not to do on Your Website

We've presented you with a lot of options to consider when building your site. But, bear in mind that less is more. A customer will not spend endless amounts of time on your site, so choose what you will specifically present carefully. Or, if you want to include lots of information and visuals, consider lumping information together.

Avoid information overload. A website can be a bit like a book—specifically a reference guide, like an encyclopedia. A reader who is researching information on Texas may read the encyclopedia entry about the state and become interested in the history of San Antonio. If the reader is researching the article online, he or she may have the option of clicking on a link to learn more about that city and may become further intrigued by the Alamo, clicking on another link to learn more about its history. However, someone else who begins to read an article about Texas may be interested in other things, such as the history of the oil industry, the economy of Dallas-Fort Worth, or the climate. Because of this, it may not make sense to provide detailed information about the Alamo in the broader article about Texas.

Similarly, on your own website, you should provide enough information on your homepage to encourage those interested in learning more about a specific topic to click through—but be careful not to lose a potential customer with too much detailed information on your homepage about something they may not be interested in. This principle of good organization, as well as clearly identified links that appear in multiple places, is collectively called site navigation. Ensure the important stuff is presented upfront, but also make sure that someone who is interested in the details can find them easily. Consider developing a basic flowchart to help you determine what information goes where.

Don't be too flashy. While it's important to sell your business in its best light, it's also important to ensure that customers can find the information they're looking for. Some business owners get carried away adding the latest bells and whistles to their websites just because they can. You may believe it's important to open with a visual and audio experience. We've all seen an example of a website that opens with a beautifully compelling series of pictures and short video segments that fade in and out or move about the screen accompanied by beautiful audio. While this may indeed create a memorable experience, there are several reasons you should consider not embedding your site with fancy flash graphics and sound. First, not all browsers support these graphics. Second, not everyone who is visiting your site wants to engage at this level or wants to sit through a time-consuming opening sequence just to get to a phone number. Third, some people will access your site from locations in which music is inappropriate and may not be able to quickly locate the option to remove sound. And fourth, search engines cannot read letters printed in flash or in graphics, which can make some core information on your website invisible to Google, Yahoo, Bing, and other search engines.

Some of the world's most popular sites are incredibly simple in their design. Craigslist appears to be exactly what it is, a simple online version of a newspaper classified section. There are no fancy graphics or even photos on its home page. And yet it attracts more than fifty billion page views a month. The basic version of the Google homepage contains the word "Google," a text box, and two buttons. Sometimes a minimalist approach is best.

Closing the Deal

Once you get a customer to your site, you should attempt to close the sale. This means providing a compelling reason to purchase something online, visit your location, or at least call you for more information. Try offering the customer a special online deal, encouraging the customer to take advantage of low traffic days/times, or informing the customer of specials. Specific offers can be compelling, particularly if what you provide is offered for a limited time, only during certain days or times, or only to online customers.

Creating your Website

There are two general options when it comes to

creating a site. You can create the site yourself or hire an individual or business to create one for you.

Do It Yourself

Until relatively recently, a website developer needed some fairly technical training to develop, host, and manage a website. Today, there are a growing number of all-in-one online website-building services that enable you to create a professional looking website with only basic computing skills. These services generally offer a broad assortment of templates, which you populate with text and pictures to create the pages of your site. The service will typically also host the site for you and allow you to update the site as often as you wish—ideal if the links, features, or other relevant information will change frequently.

This option is not ideal for all business managers, particularly those who want to create a truly custom site or do not have the time to devote to updating a site themselves. However, this will almost certainly be the least expensive option for those who simply want an online presence.

Hire Someone

This is the way to go if you'd like a truly custom site. There are plenty of individuals and companies that offer website creation and hosting. These providers vary greatly in level of experience, service quality, and price. The good ones will work with you to understand what you want to accomplish with your site and make informed recommendations for enhancements that you often hadn't considered. They'll develop a site that meets your objectives, is professional and engaging, provides important information, and is simple to navigate. They'll continue to work with you to update the site as required and should explain the entire process to you and agree on all costs upfront. Naturally, this won't relieve you of the need to make decisions yourself regarding information and site presentation (just as you would with the design of your own business).

When selecting a potential provider, always ask to view relevant examples of work and, of course, ask for a few references. Draft a quick brief of what you'd like to accomplish, and bid the business to a few potential providers. Negotiate ongoing hosting fees (and ensure you ask to have this included in your bids)—hosting is inexpensive in today's world but is often considered a significant profit center for web developers.

Expenses

The broad categories of expenses involved in developing and managing a website include:

- Creating and maintaining the site: typically the largest expense
- Search engine optimization: periodically reviewing and managing your site so it rises to the top of "natural" search results (explained more below)
- Reporting: if you choose to collect information, names, etc. from your site

- Hosting: paying for the space on a server that stores the site information and allows access to that information

- Merchant services fees: if you decide to sell items on your site (you may or may not be able to use your existing merchant account for this purpose—online fees may be a bit higher than offline fees)

Search Engine Optimization

How do you ensure that your website gets discovered by lots of potential customers? One way is to advertise your site online (as discussed in the next section, Online Advertising). Another way is to ensure that your site is likely to come up on the first page of results when a customer uses a search engine (e.g., Google, Yahoo, and Bing). This is referred to as a strong "natural search result," which contrasts with a paid search result. A paid search result appears in the text advertisements that you'll typically see on the left-hand side of any search result page. Natural search results are the non-sponsored results that a search engine returns when you type in a particular search term.

When people type a word or phrase into a search engine, the engine returns links to pages that represent the most relevant results. How does the search engine determine what's most relevant? Honestly, only the technical experts who work for the search engines know for sure. The algorithms these search engines use to determine what's most relevant to users are closely kept secrets for several reasons, not the least of which is, if people knew exactly how these algorithms worked, they could game the system and ensure their own websites come up first—when in reality the user may be looking for something entirely different.

Although the specifics of search engine algorithms are closely guarded corporate secrets, some basics are pretty widely known. For example, a site is more likely to come up toward the top of your search results if that site gets a lot of traffic, has many other sites linking to it, mentions the specific word or phrase you typed in many times, and is updated frequently. As a result, an entire industry has sprung up of online professionals who claim to be able to move your site up in the rankings based on this widely known information. This practice is known as search engine optimization (SEO)—the art of optimizing your website so that it ranks highly in natural search results. Some individuals and companies have great success with this; others do not.

If someone is designing your website for you, it's probably worthwhile to ask them about this service. Certain elements of SEO can be done once, as your site is set up, and other elements require regular updates. If online sales are a big component of your business model, it may be worth the expense to hire an expert to help you optimize your site regularly. If not, you may want to optimize the site only once, when it's initially developed.

Website Summary

- A website is the online face of your business. It should present both compelling and vital information about you in a way that's easy to navigate.

- Don't provide too much information upfront. Enable customers to easily navigate to the information they find most relevant. Also, carefully consider whether you want to use flash graphics and sound on your site.

- You can hire a firm to design and develop your site, or you can do it yourself with online tools. Many services exist today that make designing and hosting your site nearly as simple as creating a PowerPoint document.

- Developing the site is only one of the expenses you'll need to consider. Others may include hosting, reporting, SEO, and merchant services fees.

- You should consider developing your site so customers searching for relevant terms in key search engines like Google can find you easily and consistently.

9

ONLINE ADVERTISING

Overview

There are two broad types of online advertising—search and paid ad placement—and many subcategories within each. Basically, search (or keyword) advertising is managed by the core search properties (e.g., Google) and consists of a headline, several lines of text, and a link, all of which will appear only when a potential customer searches for specific words/terms that you've paid for. Paid ad placement covers a broad range of paid advertising and more closely resembles traditional print or TV advertising. This includes things like banner advertising, video roll, and pop-ups. With the rapid evolution of all things "online," this can be one of the most dynamic and potentially confusing marketing vehicles.

Search Advertising

As discussed briefly in the Website section, when a customer types a word or phrase into a search engine like Google, the search engine returns a list of web pages. In addition to these pages, most search engines will provide the customer with relevant text advertisements. These paid ads work a bit differently from "natural search" results, because the order of placement from top to bottom is determined by a combination of how much the advertiser pays and the number of customers who have actually clicked on the ad.

On Google, these ads may appear in several places on a search results page. Paid ads may appear at the top or bottom of the page among other searches or they may appear to the right of the normal search results.

Vitamins on Sale
(Ad) www.vitaminhousesam.com ▼
Always the best vitamins for less
Free shipping on all orders

Vitamin - Wikipedia, the free encyclopedia
https://en.wikipedia.org/wiki/Vitamin ▼
A vitamin is an organic compound and a vital
nutrient that an organism requires in limited...

Free Vitamins
www.startwelvite
Start your plan
today and stay well

Vitamin and Mineral Supplement Fact Sheets
https://ods.od.nih.gov/.../list-VitaminsMineral...▼
Professional guide to vitamin and mineral
supplements, presented by Office of Dietary

Free Delivery
www.doorvite▼
Start saving today
with this code

Only Organic Vitamins
(Ad) www.naturebestvitex.com▼
Get a 30 day supply or organic vitamins
when you start a health plan today.

See your ad here>

Google is currently the dominant market player for search. According to a 2015 comScore report (considered a gold-standard for online traffic measurement) approximately 65% of all searches in the United States are done on Google followed by Microsoft sites (e.g. Bing) at a rather distant 20% and Yahoo at 12-13%.

Because of this dominance, this section will focus specifically on Google search advertising. If you have limited time to set up and monitor a search advertising program, you may choose to advertise on Google only (at least to begin), as this will allow you to reach the majority of your potential customers.

Before we describe *how* to set up a text advertising campaign, let's review *why* you may want to do so. There are several benefits to text advertising:

- Low/flexible start-up costs: You can begin advertising with as small a budget as you'd like. You can set minimum advertising expenses at a few dollars per day if you'd simply like to get some experience with the service. Of course, to obtain measurable results, it's recommended you spend a bit more.

- Relative ease: Google makes the process fairly easy (so it lures more advertisers). Setting up some text ads that are triggered by a few keywords can be done quickly, even by a first-time user. However, as with anything, you can certainly invest more time and resources into developing, testing, and reworking a more complex advertising strategy. There are agencies, and even automated programs, that will do this for you. Also, it's important to realize that doing text advertising yourself will require some time—there are several adjustments to the campaign you should make to improve efficiencies, and there are several things you must do for the campaign to remain active.

- Measurable: Many advocates cite measurability as THE key benefit to text advertising. You'll get very clear feedback on exactly which text ads and which search terms generate the best results. This allows you to invest more in the terms that are working.

- Targeted: Text ads pop up when customers have searched for a particular word or phrase. Therefore, text advertising is an informationally targeted marketing tactic. It's fairly obvious that a customer who types "fresh asparagus" into a search engine is interested in information about fresh asparagus. Text advertising enables you to target customers when they're interested in learning something specific.

- Pay per click: Unlike most forms of advertising, you pay only for an ad that a customer notices and clicks on. There's an important caveat here: if many customers do not click on your ad, Google will start displaying it less or displaying it farther down the list. You'll actually need to offer Google more money per click to get it moved back up the list or displayed more often. This makes sense if you consider that all search engine algorithms "reward" links that are clicked on most often by moving them up the list, assuming that they're the most relevant links for a specific search term. This all works out for you in the long run as well. It's to your benefit to focus on search terms that result in a high number of "click-throughs" to your site.

Getting Started with Search/Text Advertising

Google's text advertising service is called AdWords. You can obtain specifics about the service by clicking on the Advertising Programs link at the bottom of the Google homepage. This will provide you with two main options: advertising on Google via AdWords (the text advertising program) or making money on your website via AdSense (the program that allows you as a website owner to embed advertisements on your site). Unless your site generates a significant amount of traffic, you'll probably be more interested in the first option.

The directions on Google are pretty straightforward, so rather than repeat them, we'll provide a few highlights and tips:

- Regional feature: AdWords provides a feature to geographically target your text ads to customers searching within a particular city or area. This won't work for all customers, as the Google service will only know the locations of users who have identified themselves. Still, it's better to set a regional preference to avoid serving ads to a user who lives two hundred miles away.

- Use very specific phrases: Try selecting more specific phrases—"custom sprinkler system," "outdoor heated patio," "family-friendly service"—for the best results. As you can imagine, a large number of advertisers will be interested in broad, general terms like "pizza" or "car." Because the competition for these words can be high, and many ads can appear here, Google will charge more for text ads that key off these terms. Plus, the customers searching for the most specific term are probably those who will be most interested in your business.

- Write more than one text ad: You have the option of creating a single text ad that will appear when a customer types in any of the search words or phrases you select, but you'll get better results if you invest a bit more time and create several ads, each keying off a different idea. (See the examples below.)

- Research: While you advertise, you'll also gain valuable insights about what resonates most with your potential customers. The ad that more customers click on is clearly displaying a more compelling message than your other ads. You might even consider using text ads to test what messaging is particularly compelling and duplicate the winning messaging in other advertising tactics, like print, radio, or your website.

Writing Effective Text Ads

As with any other type of advertising, you'll need to decide which important and differentiating feature of your business you'd most like to communicate. You'll also have to be concise. A Google text ad allows twenty-five characters of headline space and seventy characters for the body of the ad (two lines of thirty-five characters each). This isn't quite as bad as it seems. If you choose carefully what you want to communicate you can provide just enough information to compel interest, as shown in the examples below.

However, unlike most other forms of advertising, you won't have to settle on just one message. You can select a different headline and message for every word or phrase that a customer types in. The more relevant each message is to the specific search word or phrase, the better you'll do.

Examples of text ads:

The following shows what a few text ads might look like, depending on what you've chosen as your key differentiating benefit. This example uses a hypothetical Italian restaurant (Tuscan Italian Grill) and assumes the key selling points are the fresh seasonal ingredients, the well-trained and courteous staff, the comfortable and nicely landscaped patio, and the wine list.

Search Terms	Example Advertisement
Fresh ingredient terms: freshly made pasta, fresh pasta, fresh Italian herbs, seasonal vegetables, fresh Roma tomatoes	Seasonally Fresh Italian Food Everything made fresh— nothing ever frozen at Tuscan Italian Grill www.YOURWEBSITE.com
Staff: restaurants with good service, nice servers, knowledgeable wait staff, great restaurant service, quality servers	The Best Restaurant Wait Staff Our servers are comprehensively trained in food, wine, and service at Tuscan Italian Grill www.YOURWEBSITE.com

Patio: outdoor dining in Springfield, comfortable outdoor dining, best outdoor dining, nice weather restaurants	Comfortable Outdoor Dining Enjoy great Italian food outside on our intimate landscaped patio www.YOURWEBSITE.com
Wine List: best wine lists in Springfield, restaurants with Chianti, good sommeliers, wines by the glass, large selection of white wines	200-Item Wine List Enjoy an award-winning wine list and well-trained sommeliers at Tuscan Italian Grill www.YOURWEBSITE.com

Some of these search terms may work well, and others may not. Either way, text advertising allows you to quickly identify your winning sales pitch and focus your efforts on the related terms and ads with the best returns.

You'll also want to ensure that your website includes information about the topic that drew the potential customer there to begin with. And you'll want to send the customer to the correct page of your site. (Text ads allow you to determine exactly what page of your site the customer goes to when clicking on your link.) You may not always want to send the customer to your home/main page. If a local Ford dealership ran a text ad announcing specials on F150 pickups, the ad should probably direct to a page specific to that model or to a page outlining the specifics of the special offer.

Market research: As mentioned earlier, text advertisements have the added benefit of helping you understand what your most compelling message is, and they may end up changing your messaging in other (more expensive) forms of advertising. Indeed, some small business owners actually use text advertising as affordable market research—a means of determining what seems of interest to most potential customers—before putting greater amounts of money at risk in other forms of advertising such as radio or television.

Costs: You pay every time someone clicks on the link and visits your site. Unlike other forms of advertising, you (the advertiser) actually determine how much you are willing to pay (at least initially). This is referred to as your initial bid. The amount of money that a click will cost you in the long term will depend on numerous factors, including how often customers click on the ad and the competition for a chosen keyword. Costs may vary from ten cents per click up to several dollars for a popular search term. You should consider carefully before spending a lot of money on any given search term. If a typical customer earns your business $50 (profit, not gross) and your business gets about one customer for every ten people who visit your website in a given period of time (you can and should measure this if you're being diligent about payback), then a single click may be worth as much as $5 to you. If you do this rough math, you'll arrive at the maximum amount you're willing to spend per click.

Banner Advertising

A second form of online advertising is banner advertising, which is more similar to traditional print advertising and comes in many different shapes, sizes, and formats. These banner ads may be "static" or may contain moving or changing images. A good banner ad will catch the customer's attention and communicate a single message clearly and concisely. Banner ads typically appear on sites that generate a lot of traffic, like a local magazine or newspaper site.

Banner ads come in many different types, sizes, and placement. Some appear at the top of the page while others may be smaller and appear along the side next to some content (like the example on the next page). Others may be tiny "buttons" or simple sponsor call-outs.

You may decide to negotiate a rate directly with a particular website owner (for example, a local newspaper or magazine publisher), or you may use an "ad server," which is a business that provides advertising to a number of websites. For many local business owners, the best option may be to contact the most relevant websites (as there typically aren't a lot of relevant, high traffic sites in a specific area) and negotiate advertising with those sites directly or through an online advertising agency or media purchasing agency.

Sun City Sentinal (web edition)

News   Local   Sports   Business   Entertainment   Weather

Sun City Couple Wins Lottery

Andrew Jackson, Staff Writer
1:30PM January 25

They might be the luckiest couple in the country.

Jeff and Barbara Wright are the co-winners of the recent, record-breaking jackpot. And even more amazing, the couple lost the ticket shortly after purchasing it.

The couple purchased the ticket at their neighborhood grocery store and misplaced it shortly after arriving home. It wasn't until Barbara was watching the news and saw her lucky numbers come up that they began a mad search for the missing ticket.

"We found it under the dog's bed," Jeff explained. "It was chewed, but still legible."

BANNER AD

Banner Costs

The two main components of banner advertising costs are:

- Banner creation/artwork: This is typically handled by a graphic artist or online agency. Most commercial artists today can design a banner ad. Usually, the cost of generating this artwork is fairly low. You can probably find a graphic designer who can generate the type of ad you're looking for on an outsourcing site like Upwork or 99designs. When you find a potential graphic designer, tell him or her what you're looking for specifically and be sure to ask for samples of previous work.

- Advertising: Most large sites such as a local newspaper or city magazine site will have a link at the bottom of the homepage for potential advertisers. Similar to print publications, these websites will typically have a published rate card that lists advertising fees. These fees will vary depending on the size and position of the banner. A large ad on the main page will cost more than a smaller ad on a more specific area of the site; this is to your advantage, as you'd rather advertise to someone who is searching for specific information anyway. Other readers are simply wasted money. If a rate card is not offered online, call and ask for one. Also be sure to ask about a discount for first-time advertisers. A website may charge you for a set period of time or for a number of views, which is the number of times someone looks at the page that contains your ad. A key thing to remember is that a view doesn't necessarily mean a customer has seen your advertisement, particularly if the ad appears in an area where the viewer needs to scroll down the page to see it. The best way to pay a site is by "click-throughs," which refers to the actual number of times a customer clicks on your ad and goes to your website. This is also called "pay for performance." By doing this, you don't particularly care where your ad appears on the site, as you're paying only for those customers who visit your own site.

Other Types of Online Advertising

There are many ways to creatively reach a potential customer online, with new ways being invented every day.

We'll discuss a few of these and provide some guidance relevant to the small business owner. Because there are so many creative ways to reach customers online and change is so frequent, we've included a robust section on our accompanying website with more information and relevant links related to these and other services.

Social Networking/Social Media

You might consider setting up a Facebook, +You, or Myspace page for your business, which enables loyal customers, or merely the curious, to learn more about your business, add your business as a friend, or "like" your business.

Facebook and other social media are two-way communication vehicles. If you do set up a Facebook page, bear in mind that customers will be able to post any message they'd like on your page (assuming you haven't disabled this feature). In the best cases, these messages will be glowing reviews of your business that others see and respond to with positive comments of their own. In the worst case, a customer who has had a negative experience with your business may post a detailed account of his or her opinion on your page.

If this happens, you'll be faced with a public relations issue and may wonder exactly how to respond. A response that seems overly defensive or one that ignores the issue entirely may be worse than no response at all. Sometimes fans of your business will come to your defense without being prompted, but sometimes they won't. Regardless, ignoring the issue is probably not the best strategy. Thank the customer for their feedback, tell them you will take measures to ensure they have a better experience next time, and possibly offer them something to entice them back. Avoid sounding overly defensive or critical.

Because Facebook can generate very sensitive PR situations, you should carefully consider whether you have the time and expertise to manage your page before you set one up. Some businesses actually invest more time and energy in their Facebook pages than they do on their websites and all other marketing vehicles.

On the plus side, social media can be a strong word-of-mouth marketing vehicle. As customers "friend" or "like" your business, other potential customers will be exposed to it, because the friend notice will be forwarded to that customer's network of contacts. This may prompt entirely new customers to investigate.

If you do set up a social networking page, you should update your page with relevant and timely information, which helps drive top-of-mind awareness and loyalty among frequent customers. Make sure to provide a link to your actual website, which will typically offer a much richer experience and more information. You'll also want to check in regularly to see what types of comments people are making about your business and address negative ones quickly. You can also establish a "group," which allows people to sign up as fans on Facebook, but the opportunity to include information is more limited.

Examples of social media used effectively:

Restaurants can take advantage of people's natural inclination to discuss restaurants and food to their advantage. They can also take advantage of the fact that dining is a social event. Examples:

- Encourage diners to "friend" you on Facebook. Post nightly/weekly specials to your site, which will in-turn appear on your customers feed. Post anything else that you believe is relevant to their decision to dine with you, but be careful about posting too often or posting something that may be of interest to you but not a customer. While this helps you stay top of mind, the moment these posts are no longer useful to your followers, they're likely to stop following you.

- Offer UNIQUE specials only to those who follow you on Facebook, Google+ or any other site. This may provide enough value for them to follow you online and CONTINUE to follow you.

- Offer unique specials to your followers that encourage them to bring friends. Consider group specials (e.g. complimentary appetizer or dessert to parties of four or more).

- Recognize your loyal friends and encourage them to bring others in the process by offering a special birthday treat.

- Post monthly recipes.

- Post wine or beer recommendations.

Mobile Advertising

With the growing use of smartphones, mobile advertising has become a real possibility. Before considering investing in mobile advertising, you'll want to have a good sense that your area has fairly high smartphone usage or that your potential customers use these devices regularly. Maybe your customers are a bit more upscale or tech savvy than the average customer.

It used to be that people browsed normal websites on their smartphones. However, because not all websites are optimized for tiny mobile screens, it has become much simpler to download programs that are specifically designed for smartphones, collectively called smartphone applications or "apps." Apps are created to do specific things like provide travel, weather, or financial information, or to play games.

There are several ways you can ensure customers using smartphones are aware of your business:

- You can advertise directly on mobile-optimized sites or on apps via small banner ads. This type of advertising is fairly new, and the results are uncertain so far.

- You can ensure your business is listed on business ratings services like Yelp or mapping services like Google Maps. Customers use these to search for businesses.

- You can develop an app of your own. However, unless you can come up with a particularly interesting or useful program that customers will be willing to download, this may not be the best investment for a small business owner. If you go this route, you'll need to find someone who can program an application for one or both of the main mobile operating systems, Droid (Google) and iOS (Apple).

Business Rating Services

There are several online business rating and review services, including sites like Yelp. Because people who visit these sites are specifically searching for businesses like yours, it may make sense to pay one or more of them to make your business a "featured" business, thereby getting it displayed more prominently. At a minimum, ensure the information they have for your business is correct. Offer to update the information if it's inaccurate.

As with social media, you may come across negative reviews of your business on these sites. You may or may not be allowed to comment on a negative rating, depending on the service's rules. If you do comment, treat the situation delicately. Thank the customer for their feedback, ensure them you will take measures to provide a better experience next time, and consider offering them something to entice them back. Avoid sounding overly defensive or critical. In extreme cases, angry or defensive responses by businesses to these types of reviews have gone viral or even been featured by the local media. Although seeing these reviews in print can be very difficult to the typical business owner, responding indelicately can often make matters worse. See examples of how to handle negative reviews in the "Word of

Mouth" chapter.

E-mails

Unsolicited e-mails, known derogatively as "spam," have become one of the most hated online marketing vehicles. This and the adoption of better anti-spam filtering software, as well as the non-targeted nature of most e-mail services themselves, has resulted in a very low spot on the recommendation list for e-mail advertising. A much more targeted way of using e-mails as a marketing tool is to send newsletters only to customers who specifically request them. This is called "opt-in" e-mailing or relationship marketing.

While this isn't a very good way of attracting new customers, it can be a way to build loyalty among existing fans of your business, particularly if you use the e-mails to make subscribers aware of upcoming specials, events, or discounts. (Refer to the examples in the social media section). Bear in mind that even these messages might be filtered out by many e-mail systems, so you'll want to tell subscribers to add your business to their e-mail address books. This way, your messages will land in their inboxes and not their junk mail folders.

Online Couponing

As you might imagine, offering a coupon online can be tricky. If not done carefully, it's possible for customers to print many copies or forward the coupon to friends. Before you know it, you may end up with many more coupons circulating than you intended. Of course, maybe you're OK with this. If not, you can mitigate this risk by making the coupon available for a short time or making the expiration date a week or two away. Ultimately, coupons, like any type of discount, can be abused and can cheapen your company's image and should therefore be used sparingly. There are online destinations that specialize in offering coupons for limited periods. Some will even monitor results and limit the number of coupons printed.

Blogs

Blogs can be a good source of information for those who follow them regularly and can be a good means of driving loyalty among existing customers for business owners who have a lot to say and plan to put a good deal of effort into updating a blog regularly.

However, unless you have something truly compelling to say to your customers regularly that includes more than simply updating weekly special offers, it's unlikely this effort will provide you with a great return. If you'd like to keep in touch with customers, you're probably better off sending the occasional e-mail (or regular mail) to those who sign up for your newsletter or simply updating your website.

If you do want to invest the time in creating a blog, consider what aspect of your business is of most interest to customers. These may include:

- Specials
- New products/services
- Education (relevant to your offering)
- Events and news

Twitter

Twitter is really a very specialized version of a blog and is therefore also sometimes called a "microblogging" service (messages are limited to 140 characters). Therefore, our advice on using Twitter is the same as our advice about blogs in general. You'll want to invest in setting up a service like this only if you have something to say regularly to your customers and, more importantly, your customers are interested in hearing it.

Online Advertising Summary

- There are many ways to advertise your business online including search, banners, and other less traditional but growing vehicles.
- Search advertising is one of the most common advertising vehicles for small businesses and consists of text advertisements that accompany search results on key search engines like Google, Yahoo, or Bing.
- Banner advertisements are small graphical ads in a variety of formats that appear on partner websites.
- Other types of advertising include social networking, mobile advertising, business rating services, e-mails, online couponing, blogs, and Twitter.

10

OUTDOOR ADVERTISING

Overview

Outdoor advertising differs from more traditional vehicles such as television, print, or online, which are encountered primarily inside the home or workplace. While not everything in this category may be truly "outdoors" it's helpful to think of this category as all things that are encountered while out and about. There are several main types of advertising in this category:

- Billboards: The most famous example (and largest revenue generator) of outdoor advertising are traditional billboards. It's estimated that approximately 75% of billboard advertising is done by local (as opposed to national) advertisers.

- Street advertising: this is advertising added to any permanent street fixtures, including bus stops/shelters, phone booths, park benches, etc.

- Transit advertising: This advertising appears in and on mass-transit vehicles such as subways, busses, and taxis.

- Nontraditional: Because there are so many other opportunities to reach customers outside the home, we've added a general nontraditional category to accommodate everything else, including large venues such as sports stadiums and smaller opportunities like public restrooms.

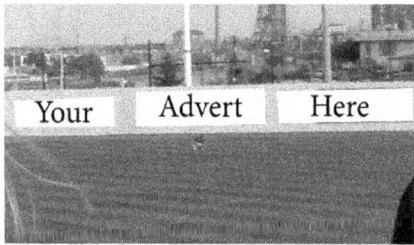

When Does It Make Sense?

For the small business owner, placing an ad in a prominent location near the business itself may make a great deal of sense. Doing so can serve four broad purposes:

1. Location: Outdoor advertising is very location specific. You'll likely be able to find a suitable ad location close to your business. (Whether the ad space is currently available is another matter.) Because much of a small-to-mid-sized business's draw typically comes from a relatively close geographic area, the location-specific

nature of this advertising vehicle means you'll be targeting customers most likely to patronize your business.

2. Reminder: A billboard or other form of outdoor advertisement has the added benefit of being seen frequently by those who live in or commute to the area. Even if a local is already familiar with your business, this has the benefit of keeping your business top of mind, thereby helping increase the customer's repeat rate.

3. Right place, right time: Because an outdoor ad is in the same area for some time, it has the added benefit of being more likely to appeal to someone who is in the right frame of mind to make a purchase. A potential customer may have passed your advertisement for twenty days straight, but on the twenty-first day, for whatever reason, that same customer may be in the mood to purchase for the first time. And for the first time, your advertisement may capture his or her attention and drive the desired action.

4. Visual message: Outdoor advertising is a great opportunity to show an image to the world. What image represents your compelling point of difference best?

The Message

There are many things competing for your potential customer's attention while he or she is outdoors. Billboards on busy roads are competing for attention with the kids in the backseat and the guy who just slammed on his brakes a few yards ahead. In the midst of this chaos, your customer may glance up and see a billboard advertising your company.

You have those few seconds to convey a message.

A billboard is similar in some ways to a magazine ad. Both are trying to capture someone's attention in a few seconds. The trick is to extend the customer's attention for a bit longer with an ad that is interesting in some way and then communicate your message quickly.

As mentioned above, outdoor advertising is a visual medium. This means you'll want to devote the vast majority of ad space to a picture that creatively tells a compelling story about your business. Use words sparingly. Show a visual that depicts the primary selling point for your business and your company name and logo as appropriate. But also include your location or contact number. Location information should be stated simply (e.g., This Exit, Smith Road, Southland Mall, Next to the Park), because a full address will not be written down and probably won't be remembered. You also don't want it to distract from your primary message.

Examples of things you may want to depict on a billboard (or other outdoor space):

- Primary message in a visually arresting way:
    - Show the food
    - Show the dining area
    - Depict customers in your target audience enjoying themselves in your restaurant.
    - Consider showing the OUTSIDE of your restaurant so that customers will recognize it when they see it (they are probably driving after-all). But only if

---

an image of your restaurant can help sell the service. In other words, if the outside of the restaurant looks appealing in some way.

- Business name and graphic/logo as appropriate
- Location—think of the simplest way to depict your business location, one that customers will register instantly:
  - If your building itself is a landmark or particularly memorable, show it!
  - Exit number
  - Main road
  - Proximity to common attraction
  - Mall or commons area
  - Include a very simple map with clear landmarks if the location is one or two turns away from the advertising site
- Contact information:
  - For your phone number, consider using letters if possible—even if it's just for part of the number
- Call to action:
  - Make a reservation today!
  - Try our famous ice cream burrito dessert tonight!

Producing the Advertisement

Most of the same agencies and graphic artists that can produce print ads can also produce outdoor ads.

However, because outdoor is a slightly different medium, you may be better off searching for an agency that has some specific experience in this space.

Typically, a creative agency will generate the graphic and forward it to the company that owns the ad space. The company that owns the space will contract with the individuals who physically apply the graphic to the board.

Buying Ad Space

As any street vendor will tell you, there's nothing new about the principle of focusing your sales efforts on locations where lots of people congregate. What's different today is the fact that the "ownership" of these spaces is increasingly consolidated among several large advertising companies. These organizations have either paid to erect signs or have paid local property owners or municipalities for the rights to advertise in certain spaces with the intent of reselling this space to advertisers. As a result, it's often easiest to start with these organizations when looking for local advertising venues. We've provided links to all of these groups on our website.

Obviously, it may be easiest to simply search your particular geographic area for available space and call the number that's included there. Look for empty billboards, public transit benches, or waiting areas that have advertisements that say something like "See. We caught your attention! Outdoor advertising works! Call us for more information."

Even if the space(s) you consider ideal is being used by another advertiser, don't give up. The advertising term may be expiring soon. If the owner of the space knows someone else is interested, the cost of the space for an existing advertiser may be more likely to go up during the renewal period, resulting in that advertiser's pulling out. You may be able to reserve space in advance. Finally, even if the ideal space is taken, the space owner may be able to suggest another location that will work. The space owner will typically be more than willing to provide you with site traffic information, so you'll have some sense for how many people will see your ad and you can compare it to any other spaces you may be interested in.

Types of Advertising

There are many different types of outdoor advertising. We will discuss some of the most popular here.

Billboards

While not permitted in all areas, including the entire states of Maine and Vermont, billboards are by far the most common form of outdoor advertising and are most frequently used by local businesses as opposed to national advertisers. Billboards are powerful for all of the reasons listed in the beginning of this section.

Billboards will sometimes offer unique opportunities for creative messaging. Some apartment complexes point out for the frustrated commuter how short the typical commute is from their property to the city. A billboard might be a particularly nice time to highlight how quiet a car's interior can be. Radio stations will sometimes advertise on billboards because they know drivers are often channel surfing as they drive. Restaurants advertise because they know evening commuters are often thinking about dinner. Businesses of all types might advertise an easy-to-remember phone number so commuters can call and order something while they drive—provided, of course, there's a good reason to call. Businesses with locations close to the physical advertisement itself will provide simple directions on how to get there (e.g., This Exit) or, if applicable, will even draw an arrow that points the way to the location.

Street: Bus Shelters, Subways, Benches

If your business is located in an area serviced by mass transit, this may be a good option. Many local municipalities use advertising as a means of supplementing city revenue. Sometimes the city manages this advertising itself, and sometimes it will contract it out to a local or national advertising manager (like Clear Channel). Either way, most advertising locations—even those that already have advertisers—will provide you with contact information. Or simply call your local transit operator for information.

These advertising venues provide most of the same benefits that billboards do, and similar messaging tends to work. One key difference is that a potential customer may have more time to read an ad while waiting for a bus then while driving a car on a busy highway. You'll still want to highlight your key benefit simply and clearly, but you could also include more specifics, like a phone number, address, and products or services offered.

Transit: Busses, Trucks, Subways, Cabs

Transit advertising is a mobile advertising vehicle. It may make sense for the same reason that street advertising makes sense, but there are some additional considerations. For example, because a bus is mobile and may cover a broad service area, it may pass through the area that your business services but may also range well beyond it. Therefore, an advertisement on a bus may not be as geographically targeted as one on a bus stop.

If interested, be sure to ask about vehicles servicing specific areas or routes. You don't want your advertisement to appear on a bus that services a route on the other end of town.

Nontraditional

Advertising can be a valuable source of revenue for nearly anyone whose property is seen by many potential customers. While some consider this a symptom of a customer culture run amok, it also represents a great opportunity for the local business owner. Even if a local property does not currently offer advertising, an innovative and creative business owner may be able to convince someone to make an exception if a particular location is perfect. A location could be perfect if it's close to your business or in a place that puts a potential customer in a particularly receptive state of mind. Restroom advertising may be a perfect place to advertise for plumbers, handymen, cleaning services, doctors, and anyone else with a creative, appropriate message that makes a customer think about your business in a new way.

Opportunities in this space are abundant. Advertising options include, but are not limited to:

- Sports stadiums: Is your potential customer likely to be a sports fan? Advertising in national team stadiums can be expensive, especially for a business that doesn't service the entire area, but there may be opportunities to advertise in smaller stadiums, like those servicing farm teams, colleges, or even local high schools.
- Plane banners, blimps, balloons, skywriting: these forms of advertising still have a unique appeal to some and can be particularly effective during the spring and summer, when people are more apt to be outdoors.
- Restrooms (public, restaurant, bar, other high-traffic): This can be particularly effective if you can find a relevant way to use it. Imagine a local home-cleaning service advertising the following message: "If we can clean this space, we can clean yours."
- Mall kiosks: these opportunities are particularly beneficial to businesses located within the mall premises.

- Outdoor maps or related informational signs: opportunities here can range from traditional advertisements on the back of a local map to including a callout for your business on the map itself with an arrow indicating its location.

- Local information booths: often located in areas frequented by nonlocals, such as tourist locations, points of interest, and public transportation hubs, information booths can provide the opportunity for local businesses to distribute banners, cards, or other forms of advertising.

- Walls: It's possible to put an ad anywhere. If there's a particularly visible, blank wall in a perfect location, it doesn't hurt to ask the owner whether they'd be interested in allowing you to post an ad in the space. It will help if you've done your research and are willing to pay a rate that's comparable to what a billboard owner might earn.

- Mobile billboards: Several companies have installed billboards on the backs of trucks that they drive around cities during times of high motor or pedestrian traffic. Some companies even pay customers to "wrap" their personal automobiles with advertising messages. While these may initially seem like good opportunities, consider that these vehicles drive along with traffic, rather than remaining stationary, which may limit the number of potential customers who see them.

- Projection advertising: Ideal for some locations that do not have existing billboard space, projection advertising enables you to project an advertising message onto nearly anything, provided it's a relatively clean space.

Often (but not always), this will limit your advertising to evening and night.

Outdoor Summary

- Outdoor advertising comes in three main forms: billboards, street advertising, and nontraditional forms, which encompass nearly any other out-of-home space.

- Outdoor advertising is very popular among small-to-mid-sized regional businesses because it can cost-efficiently target customers in a specific geographic area.

- When advertising outdoors, use visuals that graphically represent your primary benefit and include very simple directions or contact information that can be remembered simply and quickly. You typically have a matter of seconds to make an impression.

- Contact one of the large outdoor advertising companies for opportunities in your area, or simply call the number located on an ad space that does not currently feature an advertiser.

11

WORD-OF-MOUTH ADVERTISING

Overview

Positive word of mouth, referrals, or buzz should be a goal of any well-run business. Generating good word of mouth is sometimes the most effective and most difficult thing to do well. There are many businesses that haven't spent a dime on advertising in years, relying instead on customers telling their friends and family about their business.

Generally, there are two types of word of mouth: prompted and unprompted. A prompted referral happens when someone asks a trusted friend or family member for a recommendation or asks about your business specifically. An unprompted referral happens when someone talks about your business without having been asked. This typically happens when the customer has had a particularly memorable experience, either good or bad. People who say something about your business without being asked generally do so because they have a strong opinion to share!

A word-of-mouth spectrum of comments from negative (left) to positive (right) might look something like this:

Negative		Positive	
Unprompted	Prompted	Prompted	Unprompted
"I tried xyz company the other day, and it was the worst experience I've ever had. Let me tell you about it . . . ."	"Oh, xyz company? I've tried them, and they're fine but not the best in the world."	"As long as you're looking, you might want to give xyz a try. They do a good job."	"I had the best experience with this company called xyz the other day . . . ."

The internet has made it much easier to hear what others have to say about your business. Ratings sites such as Yelp, service referral sites, and industry specific sites have turned what used to be casual information passed between friends into a virtual industry. It's also now much easier for a potential customer to find out what other people think about your business before trying it—even if their closest friends know nothing about you.

Handling Negative Word of Mouth

Even if you've heard this truism before, it bears repeating: Someone who has had an excellent experience with your business may tell one other person. Someone who has a negative experience will tell five people. Perhaps many of us naturally enjoy the opportunity to complain about something. Regardless of why it happens, the first step in eliminating negative word of mouth is to provide the best product or service possible. It's also important to address product or service concerns quickly and responsibly—preferably as soon as, or shortly after, they happen. Doing so can occasionally lead to a positive referral and a more loyal customer.

But even with the best intentions, it's nearly impossible to avoid upsetting someone. As the saying goes, you can't please all of the people all of the time—and sometimes you may not want to. There are situations (hopefully rare) in which the customer has made an unreasonable demand, has acted inappropriately or abusively toward another customer or member of your staff, or committed one of the many sins we're all capable of in our worst moments.

How do you minimize the damage that occurs from these encounters—particularly when you may not even realize a negative event has occurred?

- Do a survey: You can do a formal or informal survey of your existing customers to discover what they think of your product or service. This will give you an early read on whether people are discussing any potential problems. Typically, it's not enough to simply ask a customer to rate you. Not all customers are comfortable sharing information about a negative experience. Instead, try asking the customer to give you a sense for what you could do better to improve your offering. Take this feedback seriously, avoid making excuses for any negative results, and determine how to effectively deal with it. Always start with the assumption that the customer is right and that the feedback is constructive and can be acted on. After all, the customer is only expressing a perception that has some basis in observed fact.

- Use the internet: It's always a good idea to conduct a search of your business online to see how it's being reviewed. Begin by typing your business name into a search engine to see what comes up. Also, check any sites that provide reviews in your area for negative comments. Although these sites are highly unlikely to allow you to remove reviews (this would damage the review site's credibility), no matter how unwarranted, you may have an opportunity to respond directly online. If you do so, avoid the natural inclination to post a defensive or angry response, make excuses, or blame the customer. Finally, it may be useful to set up a "Google Alert," which is a service Google provides that e-mails you when your business is mentioned in an article, blog, or similar entry.

If you do encounter negative word of mouth, a negative online post, or negative rumors in any other forum, you may choose to act, posting a carefully constructed response that's not overly defensive or critical. Acknowledge the concern, but quickly move the discussion to steps you've taken to address the problem, or highlight the many positive aspects of your business. This is a nice opportunity to reinforce your primary, differentiated benefit.

Other times, you may actually choose to do nothing. Some studies have shown that attempting to defend yourself against negative stories or unfounded rumors can serve to embed the perception more deeply with the public. Nothing aids the memory quite like repetition. Also, some fans of your business may come to your defense and post their own response.

Some experts counsel companies to focus only on the positive and promote the message you want heard. Listen carefully to the responses of politicians and notice how closely the best-trained individuals stick to their talking points regardless of the initial question.

Benefiting from Positive Word of Mouth

The best way to generate positive word of mouth is simply to offer the best possible product or service and trust that people will tell one another about it. Naturally, this isn't always easy. Many businesses exist, providing countless products and services, but not all will naturally become the subjects of positive conversation. You can increase your chances of being talked about by providing an experience or service that ranks well above expectations or that offers something new and unique to customers. You don't always have to surprise or delight every customer, but those you do will be more likely to tell others about it without being prompted.

Your key objective here is to move referrals from the prompted kind to the unprompted kind (as discussed above). Said another way, you don't simply want customers to talk about you when someone asks. You want them to bring you up unsolicited. This moves you to the top of a new customer's consideration set. Unsolicited comments are, by definition, made to friends who weren't even discussing your business.

There are several ways you can attempt to generate conversations that go on outside of your establishment:

- Get your brand out there: The more places your brand name appears, the more opportunity and reminders there will be for a satisfied customer to talk about you. This doesn't mean you have to advertise on every billboard in the metropolitan area. It means getting creative about how you might distribute items that have your brand name and message on them. Giveaways ranging from the ever-popular free T-shirt to more creative items that embody your business are often effective ways to get the conversation started. The types of people who display a product with your brand name are the types of people just begging for an opportunity to talk about you.

- Refer-a-friend offers: There are many creative ways to get existing customers to refer others. You might offer a discount good for multiple people or multiple occasions. Give it a short expiration date so it's more likely customers will give coupons to friends if they can't use them themselves. Or you may take the direct approach and simply offer a discount to an existing customer who refers someone new.

- Influence an influencer: Are there experts, industry critics, community leaders, or other people out there who serve as a natural source of many referrals? If so, reach out to these individuals. But be careful. You should realize that it's just as likely that someone may give you a negative review as a positive one. Most experts do not provide exclusively positive reviews, so it's important to be particularly confident about what you have to offer before taking this step.

- Surprise and delight: Focus on absolutely delighting one customer above and beyond his or her expectations per period (day or week). Simply doing this may pay great dividends, as that customer will share the experience with friends. Target customers who you believe are "connectors"—the types of people who feel compelled to share with others.

Some ideas for generating positive word of mouth:
<ul><li>Brand exposure<ul><li>Branded T-Shirt, glasses, plates, coasters, pot holders, aprons, or other kitchen-related items that might be shown to friends</li><li>Unique branded items that might interest customers. These might include things like a mascot or a representation of something served on the menu (e.g. a cute stuffed pig that children might play with)</li><li>Something that customers might display proudly such as a T-shirt awarded to diners who eat a menu "challenge item"</li><li>Something that highlights a unique feature of your restaurant. An example might be a coffee-table book of artwork featured in your restaurant, a branded calendar that features beautiful images of Thailand for a Thai restaurant, or a recipe book (that features recipes similar to but not exactly the same as those featured in your restaurant)</li></ul></li></ul>

- Refer a friend: encourage recommendations
  - Multiple diner offers (complimentary item for groups of four or more)
  - Complimentary birthday dessert/birthday party hosting for children
  - Wine or food tasting events
  - A creative promotion that enables diners to pay in advance for a friend's dinner, drinks, appetizer or dessert
- Influence the influencer: Reach out to/provide enticing offers to:
  - Food critics (an obvious one that we couldn't leave off)
  - Local magazine or newspaper writers and editors
  - DJ's or television personalities
  - Caterers
  - Local bloggers (food bloggers, "Mommy" bloggers, local vacation writers, etc.)
  - Local hotel concierge or similar staff
  - HR rep at a large local employer (who may make recommendations to visitors)
- Surprise and delight
  - Set aside special reserve bottles of a particular wine, cheese or something similar for your best customers which they can take advantage of at any time. Your customer may use this as a sure-fire way to impress a group of friends.
  - Offer special seating in a reserve section for your best customers. Or set this aside

> for diners that appear to be dining with you on a special occasion.
>
> o Have your wait staff occasionally suggest "off menu" items to customers who appear picky or have special dietary needs.
>
> o Encourage the chef or owner to occasionally make the rounds to chat with guests, discuss the meal or anything else of interest.

Word of Mouth Summary

- Unprompted or unsolicited word of mouth occurs when customers feel particularly passionate about a negative or positive experience.

- Be proactive about negative word of mouth. Try to determine via survey if there's a likelihood that negative perceptions exist, and carefully address any negative comments you find on the internet in a friendly, confident, non-defensive manner.

- Drive opportunities for positive word of mouth by getting your brand out there, creating refer-a-friend opportunities, influencing influencers, and surprising and delighting your best or most potentially vocal customers.

12

EVENT MARKETING

Overview

For some businesses, a good way to generate awareness and interest is by participating in a widely publicized event with a large attendance. Events have the benefit of generating interest beyond those customers who might normally frequent your business. It compels existing customers to tell others about it—potentially inviting a friend or two to participate with them. And it may get existing customers to become more loyal or compel a purchase that may not have otherwise occurred.

There are two main categories of events you may become involved with: pre-existing events (as a sponsor or participant) or your own custom events.

Sponsoring an Existing Event

It's a rare community that doesn't host the occasional event. Often, there are a number of very different types of events going on at all times of the year, catering to many types of people and interests. Whether it's a race, fundraising event, cook-off, political rally, "taste of your town," holiday, children's toy drive, community fair, or music event, all events have at least one thing in common: they need sponsorship. Most events cannot exist on the revenue of participant entry fees alone.

You may choose to sponsor an existing event because it benefits a cause that's important to you or because someone you know is a key organizer. Whatever the case, an event can be a good marketing opportunity for several reasons:

- Already publicized: Others have done the legwork by promoting the event and generating a crowd of potential customers for you. You merely need to establish a positive presence at the event that provides you with an opportunity to share your key benefit with a significant number of people.
- Local: Not all events are citywide blowouts. Many events are fairly local in their draw and therefore may represent a good opportunity to reach a large number of people in your immediate geographic area at relatively little expense.
- Shared interests: Events typically are attended by people who are passionate about the theme. The fact that your

company is a sponsor can generate some fairly positive word of mouth. It can demonstrate that you and your potential customer share a key interest, often an interest directly related to your offering.

- Leave-behinds: An event may be a great opportunity to distribute marketing materials, business cards, coupons, branded merchandise, or samples.

- Meet the public: Events are great opportunities to meet a large number of people who may be interested in your offering. Some events allow you to set up a booth, but if you do so, remember that you'll often need a "hook" to encourage people to visit. Hooks may include handouts, free offers, contests, a local celebrity, or anything else that grabs the interest of passersby.

- Branded event gifts: Many events provide keepsakes to the participants. Often, these items (the most popular of which is still the event T-shirt) contain the brand names of key sponsors. These items may be kept for many years, generating countless exposure occasions for your company name and logo—for no additional marketing expense.

Of course, in addition to the positives, there are several potential drawbacks and things to watch out for with event sponsorships:

- Attendance: Not all events are well-attended. There may be many reasons for this. The event may be a fairly new, untested, first annual activity. Perhaps something unforeseen prevents a large number of people from attending (e.g., weather, negative event publicity). You'll rarely be able to recoup your sponsorship dollars simply because the event was not well-attended. After all, the event still costs money to organize, regardless of its level of success.

- Unclear association: It can be easy for the names of key sponsors to get lost in the shuffle. A sponsor's name may appear on a poorly placed banner that's never seen by many of the participants and may never be mentioned directly by any of the organizers. Chances are, even if you've sponsored an event because the cause is important to you, you wouldn't be opposed to a bit of publicity in the process. Some event organizers are better at promoting their sponsors than others, and different levels of sponsorship may result in different degrees of association. It's a good idea to attend an event you're considering sponsoring a year in advance (if it's annual) and evaluate all of these elements prior to making a sponsorship decision.

Hosting Your Own Custom Event

Certain types of businesses are naturally able to host events more easily than others—particularly those in the retail or service industries that are used to having people come to them. These businesses include bars, restaurants, and other entertainment properties, as well as retail establishments, particularly ones that are conveniently located and often visited, like grocery stores.

Events do not need to be huge, well-attended affairs to be successful. Nor do they have to occur in the real world. They may be virtual or online events. They may be contests that occur over time and are open to participation online or through the mail. If an event is well targeted, even small events can end up attracting a good number of potential customers or succeed in increasing sales and loyalty among existing customers.

There are event companies that specialize in generating events of any size or in hosting parties, competitions, contests, etc. As mentioned in the Radio section, this includes local radio stations, which will typically broadcast the event to their listeners to generate broad interest.

Regardless of the type of event you choose to generate, there are several things you should do to make the event successful:

- Publicize the event: For an event to work well, people need to know about it—preferably people who constitute your target audience. So, you'll want to advertise your event like you would any other. Sometimes you can do this among your existing customers, particularly if the goal of the event is to generate additional business or loyalty among your existing base. But you may also want to get the word out to the broader community using any of the advertising tactics discussed in this book.

- Consider partners: If it's a large event, it may make sense to find a partner to share the costs and risks. This partner can help you publicize the event, their brand name might create an additional draw for your event, they might attract a complementary stream of new customers to your establishment, they might represent a strong brand name that will strengthen your own by association, they can provide logistical support, and they may even be able to supply additional benefits, like prizes.

- Generate excitement: Even a well-publicized event does not always attract many participants, and while this may be OK to you (you may not necessarily be looking for thousands of new customers), as a general principle, you do want to generate interest among a large group. Of all the people who hear about your event, only a modest percentage will participate, and only a certain percentage of those will ultimately become paying customers. Of those customers, an even smaller percentage will become loyalists. So it pays to cast as wide a net as possible. Generating excitement is the key to doing this. The event should offer something of value to the participants: a monetary reward or cost savings, entertainment value, the ability to learn something, the ability to meet and interact with others, or the ability to obtain or experience something that would be difficult or costly to obtain otherwise (like a trip or an opportunity to meet a celebrity).

- Provide a sales incentive: The event should include a direct incentive to engage with your business and, hopefully, to make a purchase. Sometimes you can make event participation contingent upon purchasing something. However, there is a balance here. Making an actual purchase mandatory may limit the number of people who participate in the event, but it may also succeed in limiting it to the number of people who are most likely to become long-term customers. This may work well if your goal is to obtain long-term customers. But if you also have the goal of generating awareness, you may wish to open participation to a broader group of people in the hopes that they will someday become customers or will generate positive word of mouth.

- Follow up: If you've obtained contact information from your event participants, it's important to follow up with them to close the deal. Send them information about your business, coupons, discounts, or anything you've specifically promised. It's important to follow up with everyone—not only those customers you think are most promising. It's not always immediately obvious who will become a good customer and who will not.

- Measure success: How successful was the event in generating interest, participation, names for you to follow up with, sales, and future customers? You cannot directly measure success without setting some goals and objectives ahead of time. These goals should include some measure of payback. How much additional business do you need to generate to pay for the costs of the event (both direct financial costs and your time/effort)? Congratulate yourself if the event has paid you back. If not, remember that many events do not pay back in the first round. There may be ways of improving the event in the future so that it does.

- Repeat if successful: If an event has been a success, it might be a good idea to repeat it—not only for the obvious reason of duplicating great results in future years, but also because recurring events often begin to generate word of mouth, which in turn may eliminate some of the cost you'd normally spend in publicizing them, thereby increasing the payback for future events.

The types of events that will work are often very specific to the type of business.

A list of events and event types to consider:
• Local events are often terrific opportunities to serve samples of your best items. Select a local event based on attendance and the opportunity to serve food to customers who are in your target audience. And you also may try to find relevant ties to the event itself and highlight them. For example, you may feature healthy foods loaded with vitamins to participants of athletic events like 5k runs.
• Host a wine, beer, cheese, or similar tasting event.
• Host a food-appreciation event such as a sushi preparation event, chili cook off, or spicy wing competition.
• A restaurant featuring a certain ethnic, cultural or regional cuisine may feature a speaker, author, photographer, or expert on the country, region or culture for a night of relevant entertainment and information. Similarly, the restaurant may even sponsor, discount, or simply help organize a trip to a particular region.
• Host an informative event on a cause-related topic of interest to the restaurant that

> resonates with the type of people that dine there – such as an event about sustainable farming, local sourcing, types of fish and seafood, etc.

Event Marketing Summary

- Events can be good awareness and trial-driving vehicles.

- There are two broad types of events you can participate in: pre-existing events (typically as a sponsor) or your own custom events.

- Pre-existing events allow you to benefit from the broad publicity efforts of the event managers and target local customers with shared interests. They also provide you with the opportunity to distribute samples and information, meet potential customers, and distribute branded merchandise.

- If you host your own event, you'll need to publicize it and generate excitement. You should provide some type of incentive to drive attendance, follow up on commitments, and measure the event performance.

13

PUBLIC RELATIONS / MEDIA RELATIONS

Overview

What do we mean when we refer to public relations? In the broadest sense, PR means maintaining a positive relationship with the public, specifically our customers and potential customers. In this sense, it can encompass all of our marketing activities because all of them together shape a company's image in the general public's mind.

But more typically when we talk about PR, we're referring to attempts to influence what reporters and other media personalities say about us, which is why it's a bit more accurate to refer to this as media relations. Media relations can be proactive, such as when a business contacts the media in an attempt to gain coverage of something particularly notable (e.g., new business opening, offering, promotion, or event), or it can be reactive, which typically happens when a business contacts reporters to provide its point of view about something—usually something potentially damaging. Examples might include an attempt to explain the implications of and your position on a lawsuit impacting your business or a particularly damaging review that has received some media coverage.

The Changing Media Landscape

Media outlets today are experiencing increasing pressure on the bottom line, driven by declining advertising revenues and competition from a more fragmented media market, including free sources such as the internet. As a result, many media outlets have dramatically cut staff in an effort to save money. Unfortunately for these media properties, the public's demand for content has not dramatically decreased. Short-staffed media outlets still must meet this demand.

Generating content for a news publication is not a simple task. News crews must be available to deploy on a moment's notice to cover "breaking news" in the field. Uncovering stories of political or corporate corruption requires time and often a great deal of effort by seasoned investigative reporters. Depending on the types of stories the media property covers, experts in specific areas must be kept on staff (or consultants hired) to understand what is newsworthy and to help clearly explain things to the public.

All of this is expensive. As budgetary pressures increase, media properties have reacted in two principal ways: increasing revenues and decreasing costs.

Increasing Revenues

In addition to content subscriptions, a significant percentage of revenue comes from advertising (often a majority, in the case of television and newspapers). These revenues will naturally drop during a recession. But, more disturbing than a recession is the increasing availability of free content on the internet, which is a long-term problem driving ad rates and overall revenues down.

This means media outlets are more reliant than ever on their advertisers for revenue. Media critics have long claimed that the relationship between the media and corporate America curtails media objectivity, often pointing to specific instances in which a local news source treated a "corporate villain" more favorably because the parent company was a major advertiser. Naturally, media companies vigorously dispute this claim.

Our intent is not to rehash this debate. However, if you do choose to advertise, an understanding of this issue will help you realize why media properties go to such pains to separate their advertising department from their reporting staff, which in turn will help you understand how it may be entirely possible that after having advertised with the local paper for years, your company suddenly becomes the subject of a negative article printed by that same publication.

Decreasing Costs

As with any business, media properties will attempt

to make operations more efficient before cutting back on expenses that compromise their core offering. However, it's inevitable that any media property facing profit pressures will have to cut back on staff.

As a result, news outlets have increasingly tried to obtain content more efficiently. One way to do so is to rely on news that comes from national sources, including national publications or wire services. While the outlet sometimes must pay for this content and will also typically keep staff on hand to edit the content or otherwise adapt it to local tastes, relying on these national sources is much more efficient in the long run. Most local papers and TV stations do not have the resources to send a reporter to cover an event in Washington or a hurricane in Florida or New Orleans, not to mention a story that unfolds overseas. They rely instead on national reporters that publish their stories on the wire.

Wire Services and Press Releases

A wire service is an agency that collects newsworthy stories for distribution to media properties that pay for a subscription. Often, people think of "the wire" as a single repository of articles, but in reality there is more than one service and collection available. Some wire services are set up by national news outlets (e.g., Dow Jones, *The Los Angeles Times*, *The Washington Post*) seeking to offset their own costs by selling stories to other news outlets. There are also wire services that release news exclusively to online sources (such as Google News, Yahoo News, and blogs).

Among the stories available on the wire are press

releases issued by companies. The overall objective of any company issuing a press release is to spread awareness of something that will ultimately benefit the company's image, sales, or profits. The specific topic of a press release can vary, as can the specific rationale for releasing it. The following are just a few of the things that might be included in a press release:

- Opening: an announcement of the grand opening of a store, outlet, factory, or other location, typically accompanied by specifics.

- New offering: an announcement of a new product, line of products, service, or similar offering and specifics as to why the offering is newsworthy.

- New name: a company will want to make the public aware of a new name or branding identity to avoid confusion and generate excitement.

- Special event: the announcement of a special event, contest, or similar event.

- Statement of position: a company may release its views on a particular policy or issue of public interest, particularly if the position is contrary to a broadly held view.

- Charity: a company may issue a release related to a large charitable donation or other community service to draw attention to an important issue and the company's role in the community.

- Hiring: if a company is hiring a particularly large number of people, it may publicize the fact, not only to generate awareness and applications but also to highlight its importance to the community.

- Sale, merger, or acquisition: to generate awareness, raise credibility, let the public know about an important relationship, or avoid confusion, a company may wish to clarify its ownership.

- Award: a company may choose to highlight a particular award or achievement.

- Anniversary: the announcement of a company, product, or event anniversary and the chance to highlight its beneficial impact on the community.

- Informational: a company may choose to release information, a how-to guide, a list of things to watch out for, or something similar to help to position itself as a trusted expert in a particular field.

How to Write a Press Release

A reporter typically is assigned to cover a newsworthy event or a topic of public interest (e.g., stories related to exercise or real estate) and will commonly conduct research on wire services or online to find material for the story. Sometimes the reporter is looking for something specific, like information pertaining to a building that burned to the ground last night. Other times, the reporter has an idea for a story he or she would like to write, like what motivates some people to stick to an exercise routine. And sometimes reporters are just "fishing"—searching the wires or the Web for recent (sometimes local) news in their areas of interest.

What they typically are NOT looking for is a story that seems too commercial or promotional. Reporters have a finely tuned sense for what constitutes "news" in the eyes and ears of their loyal viewers or readers, and they know what does not. A reporter risks appearing too commercial and thereby less objective and credible if a story consists of nothing more than an advertisement for a local business.

Releases should contain newsworthy information of interest to the general public, or, more specifically, to customers within your target audience. This doesn't mean the story must be non-promotional. It simply means the story must contain information that an unbiased reader in your target audience would potentially deem valuable.

The format of a press release should follow a few basic rules. It should include a contact name, including an address, phone number, and email at the top of the release (and should end with the same name and number). Along the top should be a concise headline that highlights what you consider to be the most important take-away. What one thing would you like someone to know, assuming that they don't go on to read the full article? Finally, beneath the headline should be a "Dateline" which includes the city, state and date of the release.

The following example shows how a short news release can provide pertinent information about a local business promotion in a way that's engaging and valuable to the average customer:

BOB'S PETS REVOLUTIONIZES HOW CUSTOMERS SHOP FOR PET FOOD THROUGH CUSTOM NUTRITION EVALUATIONS
Dateline: January 1, 20xx. Anytown, USA
Contact Name: Bob Smith
Contact Phone: 800-555-1111
Contact Fax: 800-555-2222

January 1, 20XX, Anytown, USA – Bob's Pets recently introduced what may be the answer to a pet owner's dilemma when purchasing nutritional pet food.

Bob's Pets is offering free nutritional screening, conducted in partnership with the Anytown pet clinic, to better identify the unique nutritional needs of individual pets.

"With so many nutritional opportunities out there, it can be difficult to determine exactly what your pet needs to stay healthy and energetic," says Robert Smith, president of Bob's Pets. "It's not always as simple as choosing a puppy formula or a food optimized for older dogs. With free nutritional screenings, and specific recommendations based on those screenings, we've removed the guesswork."

A traditional pet store typically carries many types of pet foods and many more vitamins and minerals developed for specific needs, including medical needs such as hip and joint difficulties, excessive shedding or allergies. While many of these products can help keep an animal healthy and happy, not all products are appropriate for every pet. Proper medical screening of a pet, including an examination and blood work when appropriate, can identify specific health care needs that an expert can translate into the best nutritional solutions for each individual pet.

Bob's Pets offers free screenings to its customers every Sunday during business hours (9 to 6). Screenings are by appointment.

"The results have been incredible," says Smith. "Since we started offering the service, we've had hundreds of people take advantage of it, and many of my customers have come back months later to tell me how much of a difference it's made in their four-legged friends' lives."

Contact:
Robert Smith
###

Restaurant Opening Press Release Example:

LA RISTRA BRINGS TRADITIONOAL SANTA FE CUISINE AND EXOTIC HIGH DESERT INGREDIENTS TO COLUMBUS, OHIO
Dateline: January 1, 20xx. Columbus, Ohio
Contact Name: Andrew Smith
Contact Phone: 800-555-1111
Contact Fax: 800-555-2222

January 1, 20XX, Columbus, OH – La Ristra is the first restaurant in Columbus that sources ingredients direct from Santa Fe and teaches its diners about those ingredients to bring an absolutely authentic Santa Fe dining experience to Ohio.

Santa Fe, New Mexico is a region that uniquely

blends the heritage of the Old West, the unique culinary offerings of the High Desert, and the traditions and delicious foods of Mexico into a dining experience that's experienced nowhere else in the country.

Andrew Smith, the owner and executive chef of La Ristra applies his 10 years of experience running a premiere, Michelin-rated restaurant in Santa Fe to the creation of a new restaurant in Columbus, Ohio. Andrew is not only dedicated to shipping food that is sourced directly from this fascinating part of the country, he's also dedicated to ensuring that the dining experience captures the ambiance of the High Desert.

"I didn't just want to offer traditional Mexican or even South Western cuisine," Andrew said. "I wanted to take things that diners already appreciate and give them a uniquely Santa Fe twist like our Bacon-Wrapped, Green Chili Snake-Bites or our Pinto, Chili, and Cactus appetizer."

The menu items at La Ristra are rich with local ingredients such as Hatch green chili, blue corn tortillas, and even touches of local game such as snake and rabbit. These items are added to traditional Southwestern favorites like chili, rellenos, enchiladas, empanadas, steaks, salads, soups, and guacamole.

"In addition to providing some great eats, we like to

*inform our diners and have a bit of fun in the process,"
Andrew continued. "Our bartenders custom design
margaritas with regional tequilas, juicy Santa Fe fruits,
and ingredients. And our wait staff is knowledgeable
about local chilies and game and love discussing these
with our diners. We've even got a few members of our
staff that were born and raised in New Mexico."*

*La Ristra is open for lunch and dinner 7 days a week.
In addition, the restaurant features Sunday brunch
with what the chef describes as the best Huevos
Rancheros outside of the Land of Enchantment. And
every Monday night the restaurant hosts a Santa Fe
tasting event with 7 samples of New Mexico sourced
chili and guacamole.*

*"Our restaurant in Santa Fe is one of the most popular
restaurants in town," says Andrew. "La Ristra is the closest
I could come to replicating the experience in Ohio without
picking the restaurant up and dropping it here. Be sure to
come by and visit us for our grand opening on January 15th
at 115 Main."*

*Contact:
Andrew Smith
###*

The information in this example press release clearly
was included to benefit Bob's Pets by making customers
aware of a new offering and to hopefully generate

incremental business for the company. However, the press release also does several things that balance the owner's commercial interest with the interests of the general public. The story promotes a valuable free offer. It provides information that the public (or pet owners) may find valuable. It draws attention to another community resource, the Anytown Pet Clinic, with which it has a partnership. Finally, it references the program's popularity, implying that the story has already been deemed newsworthy by customers of the business. The final quote provides a bit of human interest as well, making the story more personal.

As with any marketing activity, use the press release as an opportunity to communicate your primary message. The reference to your primary benefit may not be overt, but the nature of the release should make it clear what type of business you run and what its core value is to your customer. In the example above, Bob's Pets may specialize in nutritional expertise. This press release says something about the type of business customers are dealing with. Bob's Pets believes that the health of your pet is so important that it is willing to provide free health screenings to ensure your pet leads a happy and healthy life.

Once you've written your release, you'll want to put it on the wire. Links to the relevant services are included on our website. You can also contact local publications directly. Start with the editor of the business section or another section that's appropriate to the information included in your release.

You'll also want to include the release on your website in a section titled "News Coverage" or "Your Business Name in the News" wherein you also talk about which news outlets picked up the story. (e.g. On May 3, 20xx, the following article appeared in the Springfield Gazette covering the grand opening of Bob's Store.)

A list of PR ideas to consider for your business:
• Reach out to local media contact to help promote any event that you host. (See an example list in the Event Marketing section). • Offer giveaways to a radio station to encourage them to mention your restaurant to listeners or offer the giveaway as a prize for a contest that they come up with. Make sure the radio station is a fit for your target audience. • Write a press release that provides relevant and interesting information about your restaurant when it opens, moves, or even closes. • Offer to partner with a local media property to help write articles that are a good fit for your restaurant. Examples may be a monthly column on healthy eating choices. Always tell the reader that they can get more information from you or a knowledgeable representative of your restaurant.

Public Relations Summary

• Public relations or, more accurately, "media relations," is the act of a company reaching out to the media in an attempt to encourage the publication of a story related to the business. These stories may be proactive or reactive in nature.

- Because media companies face increasing cost pressure, many turn to wire services to obtain stories written by experts, reporters in other regions, or reference materials for a related story. Company press releases are typically released to these wire services and picked up by local media properties.

- A company may write a press release for many reasons. Among them are announcements (store opening, change of location, name change), educational material, or information of public value (hiring, special offers).

- A press release should include information about your business, the core reason for the release, your primary message, and any other element that makes the story newsworthy.

14

MISCELLANEOUS TACTICS: INNOVATIVE IDEAS VS. FADS

This book has been about how to leverage tried and true marketing techniques including messaging and marketing tactics that help deliver real returns. While not all of the tactics described here will work for you, they are presented because in the right circumstances, and for the right companies, they have been demonstrated to provide positive returns.

This section is about how to determine if a brand new way to reach customers – one that we may not have discussed in this book – is right for you or is simply a fad and therefore possibly a waste of money.

If you are the type of manager who takes a more conservative approach to marketing, if you tend to invest only in those activities that have specifically worked for you before, if you only invest in mainstream marketing tactics like radio or magazines, then this chapter may not be for you. We are not suggesting that this is the wrong approach. In fact, this book suggests that it is exactly the right way to go about marketing.

If, however, you like to occasionally take a risk on new marketing tactics then read on. There may be very good reasons to do so.

The Birth of New Marketing Tactics

There are plenty of reasons to try new approaches to marketing. We've highlighted many of them throughout the book. The decision really amounts to determining how best to reach your most promising potential customers.

New ways to reach customers are invented all the time. Anything that is seen or interacted with by lots of people can be monetized by the ad men of the world, and sold to you as a way to advertise.

A good, clever example of this is street advertising which we highlighted in the section on outdoor advertising. Lots of people stand at bus stops every day, often with little to engage their attention. Eventually, someone pitched the idea of selling ad space on the sides of bus stops (and busses, and subways, etc.) to cash-strapped municipalities.

Street and transit advertising isn't necessarily new. But it wasn't a mainstream advertising vehicle until a company with lots of contacts among advertisers and advertising agencies was able to connect the opportunity and the money to make it a sustainable proposition. And even then, it didn't take off until several forward-thinking companies took a risk and agreed to test the tactic, demonstrating that the investment actually worked. And even then it took lots of companies investing across lots of different cities and negotiating ad rates down to a reasonable level that ensured that the tactic was profitable, to bring the tactic into the mainstream. The evolution from a new, untested advertising vehicle to one that's mature, proven, and priced appropriately is not a quick process.

Perhaps the most dramatic example of the development and evolution of a new marketing vehicle is website advertising (or what we call banner advertising in the online advertising chapter). Banner advertising and website sponsorship moved from an over-hyped, expensive proposition in the late 90s to a mature, widely used, well-tested, and relatively inexpensive marketing tactic today.

In the late 90s and early 2000s the internet revolution (and bubble) was in full expansion mode. The media was feverishly trumpeting the emergence of a new force that would revolutionize and make obsolete entire industries. There was plenty of "evidence" at the time that anything with a dot com at the end of its name would come to dominate entire industries. We read about the astronomical investments and valuations of companies which had begun weeks ago as an idea on the proverbial cocktail napkin. Suddenly, much of our economic growth, if even just on paper, appeared to be driven by this new force. And this force wasn't relegated to the United States. It was simply centered there. It was forecast that this online force would come to dominate the world.

In public, the venture capital crowd justified atmospheric valuations for profitless companies by pointing to the value of the industries that were being disrupted. For example, it didn't matter that there were twenty online pet stores with less than a million dollars in revenue among them. What mattered was that within a few years, the multi-billion-dollar pet industry was all going to be online. And anyone who couldn't grasp that fact, it was politely suggested, hadn't been paying attention to what was going on around them.

While this story was being told in the mainstream press, there was a lesser-known story going on behind the scenes that involved an effort to justify the valuations being placed on these companies and to help determine which company among the many competing in the same market would emerge as the leader.

One of the ways to do this was to demonstrate that a base of advertisers was onboard and shared the company vision. Advertising and marketing managers at big companies were approached by media companies representing the websites, or by employees of the websites themselves, and asked to invest huge sums of money. In some cases, millions were required to become a site partner, benefits of which might include some banner ads and partner recognition.

The pitches were varied and creative. As an official site partner and sponsor, the advertiser would have early and exclusive category access to an online business that was certain to become the next BIG thing. The advertiser would beat out competitors that were all clamoring for a piece of the action. The advertiser's brand would be seen as a leader in the space and would gain the loyalty of a generation of consumers who were going to be doing everything online for the foreseeable future.

The only catch was that the millions of consumers who were supposed to be using the site had not yet materialized. And even that fact was often carefully masked by those seeking advertising support.

Many advertisers rightly wondered how they could be expected to spend $1 million dollars to advertise on a website with several thousand viewers when they could advertise on the local news and reach millions of real consumers, for a fraction of the cost.

It was clear to the Silicon Valley crowd that mainstream advertisers simply didn't get it. Hadn't these marketers been paying attention to the news? Didn't they realize that the world was shifting away from the old brick and mortar shop to the much more convenient and gleaming internet highway?

In retrospect, it's easy to be amazed at the fact that many advertisers did shower online retailers, online magazines, and even bloggers with millions. But at the time, it was very difficult to keep a rational investment mindset amid the hype. Marketers in big organizations wanted to be seen as visionary and there was pressure from senior management at many Fortune 50 firms to invest in promising new marketing vehicles. At times, it was easier to take a risk than it was to make the case for not jumping aboard the trend.

Today internet advertising is much different. The industry has matured. Metrics have been developed that tell us exactly how many people have viewed an advertisement and who has clicked on the ad to be taken to another website. We know lots about who has actually seen the ad, including demographic data and even shopping habits and psychographic details based on the other types of sites they visit.

And because many advertisers are investing in the space, and many online properties are competing for those dollars, ad rates have stabilized at a level that enables a strong return on investment. Some online ads are more expensive on a per person basis than many other marketing vehicles including television, radio, and billboards. But because they are often so targeted, and have proven themselves, it can be well worth the extra expense. When advertisers conduct detailed studies of which advertising vehicles return the greatest bang for the buck, online adverting rises to the top in many situations.

Some Tactics Simply Don't Make Sense

Despite its rocky start, online advertising eventually emerged as a valuable marketing tool. But not all marketing vehicles last.

There are many ways to generate awareness for your business and to potentially generate new customers. Many, but by no means all of them, are discussed in this book. But some simply don't make practical sense for any number or reasons.

Airplane banner advertising may make sense for some types of business at certain times of the year or in certain locations. A good example might be a bar situated in close proximity to Miami Beach which relies on business from beach-goers. Miami Beach may also make sense for airplane advertising because there is typically a large concentration of potential customers in a single location, many of which are lying on their backs in the sand looking up at the sky. But the same tactic makes little sense in Minneapolis in the middle of the winter when most people spend little time outdoors. The owner of a fleet of airplanes in Minneapolis may decide to try to generate a bit of extra revenue by convincing local businesses to advertise from the back of his planes. If anyone takes him up on this offer, it probably will not be long before they regret the decision. In short, this particular advertising vehicle in this specific city likely won't be around for long. While airplane advertising may not be a considered a "fad" everywhere, a brief introduction in the Snow Belt fits the definition nicely.

This may seem an obvious example of an advertising vehicle to steer clear of, but there are many ideas that come along that may not be so easy to evaluate. Perhaps they simply haven't been widely adopted yet. Are they the next big thing or will they be gone next year? Are they worth trying? Are they a perfect fit for your business even though they may not work for others? Is the marketing vehicle itself so new and strange that it may actually get a lot of attention?

We've listed a few hypothetical cases below. As far as we know these are fictional but similar opportunities may very well exist in the real world.

- An advertiser is able to use a projector to beam an advertisement onto a local landmark at night.
- A local concert is willing to stamp the hands of all attendees with your business name and logo.
- A local cab company tells you that they will put bumper stickers with your business logo and message on their fleet of cabs.
- Someone offers to attach ribbons with your logo on it

to the necks of swans, geese and pigeons at a local park.

How do you evaluate whether these make sense? A good first step would be to evaluate them against the targeting principles discussed in chapter two. Is the vehicle a good fit for your target audience? Are the right people likely to see it at the right time? You'll also need to consider whether the vehicle is too expensive per person reached? As discussed in the chapter on measuring results, you don't want to pay any more than the expected reach times the expected response rate times the revenue per potential customer. And it's important to remember that response rates are often much lower than you might expect.

What are some specific and crazy ideas you may consider? Well, since you ask, we've thrown a few at you that don't fit neatly into other areas. If something strikes your fancy, always remember to find a way to test with a limited investment first.

- Grocery Store: Can you partner with a grocery store to actually put your restaurant's name and logo on produce or in a food aisle that's relevant to your restaurant? The manager may see this as a conflict of interest at first, but if you offered to distribute a recipe or two at your restaurant that got the customer back to the grocery store for raw ingredients, that might serve as an enticement.
- Can you sponsor a local band to actually write and perform a song about your restaurant? What if the song became a local hit and the

> band began to play it at many different venues?
>
> - Can you sample food in a way that might be seen as a public service and might therefore get some media attention? Maybe you could offer food to stranded travelers, those stuck in traffic jams, half-time at a soccer game, people waiting in line at any big event, etc.
>
> - Can you partner with a bar, bakery, or other business that doesn't compete directly with you? Perhaps you could feature a bar's signature cocktail on your menu in exchange for the bar including your signature appetizer or dessert as a memorable snack for patrons with the munchies.

There are also tactics that may not cost much money but are more likely a waste of time or other resources. A good example of this is the QR code, short for Quick Response Code.

Developed in the 90s by the Japanese auto industry,

the QR code is simply a visual bit of code much like a UPC code that a specialized reader can decode and make sense of. The message thus revealed is typically in the form of text (many times a website URL). The QR code was seized upon by the advertising industry as a means to encode links to websites that a QR code app on a smartphone could decode, enabling the owner of the smartphone to go directly to the advertiser's website for more information.

Every marketer at a large organization was pitched the need to include QR codes on everything. QR codes could link to sites with games that would drive greater "brand engagement." QR codes were included on product packaging so that consumers could scan them in stores and learn more about the product. QR codes were included anywhere in the real world where an advertiser wanted to create a link to the online world. QR codes would link the real world and the digital world!

The only problem was that customers and shoppers saw no real reason to scan them. Many marketers and advertising firms saw QR codes as essentially a means of getting a customer to view yet another ad. The payoff was always gimmicky, "salesy" or of no obvious value. And those few customers who had actually gone to the trouble of downloading a QR scanner learned this lesson quickly. So instead of scanning QR codes, customers decided to ignore those little codes and simply go about living their lives.

The lesson is that new tools such as the QR code will only be widely used if there is a clear benefit to the end-user. Unfortunately, the QR codes seemed to be of much more value to the advertiser than the end user. It also didn't help that many people never got the news that QR readers existed. But this was driven more by the fact that early adopters found no value in the technology and so, never passed on the word to others.

You may not have heard of or ever tried to decode a QR code but you've likely heard of Twitter. At the time of this writing, nearly all Americans had at least a passing familiarity with the "micro-blogging service." Twitter is highlighted in our online marketing section.

However, despite that fact that you and nearly everyone else knows about Twitter, statistics would suggest that you probably don't use it regularly. Twitter itself does not regularly publish usage statistics, but a variety of polls find that while as many as 20% of people have actually "used" Twitter, the percent of people who use it regularly is much lower.

So is Twitter just like a QR code? If someone suggests to you that you should reach more customers through Twitter, should you listen or ignore the advice? Answering this question is not quite as easy as suggesting that you take a pass on QR codes.

In some ways, Twitter is like QR codes in that the user base is relatively low, and sometimes the true benefit of the service accrues to the sender of information and not the recipient. Many people including celebrities, news writers, and business leaders, see Twitter as a way of indulging their need for attention. Much like an aspiring blogger, many people assume that the world hangs on their every word, and Twitter provides a ready means of indulging their narcissism. And judging by their tweets, some advertisers appear to feel the same way.

However, there is a core group of people who regularly use Twitter to keep up to date on news and information that they find relevant. This may include traditional news, financial or investment related information, deals and discounts, weather, gossip, or whatever the user finds valuable. For these people Twitter is a helpful tool. It's a means of getting information quickly, the moment it is available. Twitter keeps them on top of current events, and for some, it may even be a means of staying ahead of the game – of getting information first, before the masses.

The thing to bear in mind is that, despite the attention focused on Twitter by the media (who see it as a valuable tool themselves) the actual number of regular people who frequently use Twitter is relatively small. But to these people, Twitter has become a service that they can't live without.

So, while Twitter remains one of the most over-hyped social media vehicles currently available, much like other marketing tactics, you may want to consider using it if your customer is one of the core group of die-hard Twitter users.

Beware of Marketing Experts

How can you tell if a new marketing vehicle is something like a QR code (probably not worth your time), Twitter (possibly worth your time depending upon your customer), or Facebook (a mass market vehicle that emerged into the mainstream)?

Unfortunately, the views of experts in advertising or the media are not always the best means of determining this. There are a number of reasons why this is true.

People who work in the advertising industry are

often very different than their clients who actually pay for the advertising. In some cases, advertising experts have never run a business themselves. (The same is unfortunately often true of consultants.) They don't always have a good sense for what constitutes a good investment and may not even realize exactly how to measure results. They will often speak in grand terms about the benefits of building awareness and brand equity. And while both are important concepts, the advertising expert may not understand that driving sales and profits is equally important.

Advertising agencies are incentivized to sell you advertising. They may not be selling the ads themselves, but many times their commissions are tied to advertising spend and at a minimum, if you do nothing, then they will become much less valuable to you and may ultimately lose your business. We are not suggesting that an advertising agency will actively mislead you into spending money on a truly bad idea (although it does happen). More likely, someone who works at an advertising agency will simply be a passionate advocate for the idea of advertising and its many benefits without properly understanding the associated risks that may accrue to you as a business owner. And they need you to actively market yourself to retain you as a client. They want you to succeed, but, despite that, your interests are never perfectly aligned.

Advertising experts at agencies, in the media, and elsewhere are typically passionate about their field. They stay abreast of the latest trends and typically have many contacts within the industry. They may attend conferences and seminars that highlight trends. As a result, they become passionate advocates for new ideas and tools. Often, this is because they want to look out for the best interest of their clients, readers, or viewers. But, in order to sell themselves as experts in the field, they also need to appear to be ahead of the curve. As a result, they are sometimes passionately selling the next big thing before anyone understands the true value of the investment. We've provided two examples of how this can happen above – QR codes, and internet advertising (in its early days).

Miscellaneous Tactics Summary:

- New marketing tactics are invented every day. Some will make sense for you but many will not. Your best approach is to apply a bit of common sense about whether you believe this new tool is a potentially good way of reaching your potential customers. Do an internet search and try to learn a bit about it. And then ask a few of your customers whether they use the tool or think it might be a good idea.

- Don't always trust the "experts." Many advertising agencies have an incentive to sell you on the next big thing and appear to be on the cutting edge themselves. Some have never run a business and don't properly appreciate marketing investment fundamentals.

- However, you shouldn't be afraid to try something new either. Like many ideas, some are good, some are bad, but many fall somewhere in between and simply depend more upon the quality of the execution.

- If you decide to try something new, you should always test the idea with a minimal investment of time and money first.

15

MEASURING RESULTS

Overview

Throughout this book, we've highlighted ways to identify who your most likely new customers will be (targeting), how to effectively speak to them (messaging), and which tactics to employ to reach them when they're most receptive to your message (marketing tactics). All of this is based on proven marketing principles that have been around for many decades. But even if you take great care to craft the perfect message and leverage some creative marketing tactics, there's no guarantee your investment will pay out. Or, more likely, some things may work particularly well and others may not pay back.

Or, as the marketing saying goes, "I know that half my marketing money is wasted. The problem is, I don't know which half!"

With limited money to spend, how do you ensure

that you get the best return on your marketing investment? Ensuring that your investment is a good one will require a few time-tested techniques. Broadly speaking, there are three means of accomplishing your marketing goals:

1. Ensure you know your target audience and have a clearly articulated primary message before you spend a dime on marketing tactics.
2. Measure the results of your marketing tactics after you've implemented them.
3. Optimize future investments based on what you've learned.

Start with the principle that you'll never get things perfect the first time around. (Of course, this shouldn't prevent you from trying!) The real key to marketing success is measuring your results so you know what works well, what doesn't, and where you need to improve to ensure your marketing investment is one of the most cost-effective investments you make.

Optimize Your Strategy Before Going to Market

We've already discussed the need to optimize your target audience and messaging strategies. If either of these two elements isn't working, then no amount of money spent on advertising will fix it. Said another way, if you're saying the wrong thing to the wrong people, you won't convince them to spend money with your business, no matter how often or in what way you reach them.

The first step in measuring marketing effectiveness

is to test your strategy before you spend any money implementing it. Some of these techniques have already been discussed in the Targeting section and Messaging section, but we'll repeat the basics here:

- Targeting: Look at your current customer base or the customers of one of your key competitors to get a sense for the types of people who are most likely to become future customers. The best way to broaden your customer base is to find customers who share some features with those who already like what you have to offer. Talk to your existing customers to get a sense for shared interests—the things many of them have in common that you can use to find more of them. They may have a similar age or ethnic makeup, but the more relevant factors may be personality traits that aren't too easy to see. If you need to, conduct a survey to confirm what you've hypothesized through observation.

- Messaging: What truly differentiates you from your competition? If you could say only one thing about your business, this is it. If you haven't defined this yet, ask your current customers for help. What, in their opinion, differentiates you from your competitors? Why do they choose to spend money with you? The opinions of your most frequent customers will be particularly valuable. You can do this same exercise with your competitors' customers. If you're considering offering a new product or service, ask your best customers in advance whether it's appealing to them. As you discuss your most appealing feature(s) with your customers, try to get at the core of what's most appealing. How would you summarize this in a sentence, or, better yet, a few words? Can it be summarized visually? Your customer's opinion of your business won't always match your own. This isn't necessarily bad—after all, they've chosen to spend money with you. The key is to establish why they like you and to tell even more people about it. Once you've established what separates you from the pack, you'll need to come up with the most convincing way to sell someone else. Your existing customers can be useful here as well. Test your sales pitch on some of your best customers to see if it resonates.

Measuring Marketing Results

How will you know whether your investment has worked? As a busy business owner, the temptation will be to assume that you've done your marketing job after you've created and placed an advertisement or two. However, if it's worth spending the money to begin with, it's worth establishing whether that money did its job. Here's how you do that:

1. Establish a baseline: You won't know how successful your advertising strategy is until you know what your business would have done without it. For this, you must establish a baseline. Let's say you've chosen to run a radio advertisement for one month. You'll want to know how much business you would have gotten during this month without it. This isn't necessarily as simple as assuming a typical month's sales. You'll also want to take into account, as best you can, anything else that

might have accounted for a change in sales that month, including the season (do you do better in the summer?), weather (was there a bad snowstorm this month or last month?), competitive actions (did a competitor have a big sale or did they shut down for a week?), and any other anomalies (did you get or lose some business for a reason not related to your advertising?).

2. Confirm the results: Even if nothing else seems to account for your success this month, sometimes you just don't know for certain until you ask. If you have more than one marketing activity going on at once (online text advertisement and a billboard), it may be unclear which is driving a customer to your store. Perhaps it's simply word of mouth. If a customer is a new customer, consider asking how he or she heard about you. Tell your staff to do the same thing. If it's not always immediately clear who your new customers are, tell your staff to ask that as well. (Is this your first time doing business with us? May I ask how you heard about us?) You don't have to do this all the time—just those times when you need to measure the results of a current marketing campaign.

3. Tie results to a specific promotion: When possible, try to establish a way of measuring the results of a promotion directly. Including a coupon in a newspaper ad will give you a sense for how many people read the ad, cut the coupon, and used it. Of course, not all people will cash in the coupon. You may have to guess how many people forgot to use it or simply couldn't be bothered to cut the coupon but thought your business sounded good enough to try anyway.

Calculating Return on Investment

There are a few things you'll want to consider when establishing exactly what return you got from your marketing investment. There are many objectives you may want to accomplish through your marketing efforts, including driving awareness, driving repeat business, retaining existing customers (particularly if a new competitor has opened nearby), or driving new customers to your business.

Your success against any of these marketing metrics can be measured, though some are more difficult to measure than others. Ultimately, each will rely on your establishing what the baseline would have been had you not advertised and what the new baseline is after advertising. For the purposes of this discussion, we'll assume that the objective of your marketing efforts is to drive trial, i.e., drive new customers to your business. The general return on investment (ROI) equation that we'll use is:

$$\frac{\text{Net}}{\text{ROI}} = \frac{\text{Sales After Variable Expense}}{\text{Marketing Expense}}$$

Assume then, that your average monthly sales level is \$100,000. Assume you've arrived at this figure by looking at your average monthly receipts that occur during times when you're not already advertising and there are no other external factors that may positively or negatively impact your business results. Remove any outlier months from your calculation.

Assume that subtracting all of your average monthly

expenses gives you a profit of $10,000 per month. However, the figure we really want to use for the purposes of calculating a marketing payback is your gross sales net any variable (and one-time) expenses. For the purposes of this exercise we'll treat things like rent and employee expenses as fixed (assuming they won't change in the short run). When calculating whether your marketing expense paid back, you want to subtract only expenses that are variable depending on sales levels. This is because you would have paid fixed and one-time expenses whether or not you executed your marketing tactic.

Let's consider a very simple small business profit and loss (P&L) statement:

Mary's Lemonade Stand	Avg Month
Gross Sales	$100,000
Variable Expenses:	
lemons (10%)	$10,000
cups & other supplies (20%)	$20,000
other variable (10%)	$10,000
Sales after Variable Expenses	$60,000
Marketing Expense	$0
Sales after Variable & Marketing	$60,000
Fixed Expenses:	
employees	$20,000
corner rent	$20,000
other fixed	$10,000
Profit after Variable & Fixed	$10,000

In this example, Mary's Lemonade Stand earns

$100,000 gross sales on average every month. Variable expenses are $40,000, and fixed expenses are $50,000, leaving $10,000 in profit on average each month.

Let's assume these variable expenses are truly variable, and the fixed costs are truly fixed. This would mean that if Mary earned an extra $10,000 in gross sales, she would pay an extra $4,000 in variable expense ($1,000 for extra lemons, $2,000 for additional cups, and $1,000 for other things that were needed to sell more lemonade). But she would pay no additional fixed expense because the amount she pays for rent and salaries would stay the same. So when she makes an extra $10,000 in gross sales, she makes an extra $6,000 in profit.

Mary's Lemonade Stand	Avg Month	Additional Revenue
Gross Sales	$100,000	+$10,000
Variable Expenses:		
lemons (10%)	$10,000	$1,000
cups & other supplies (20%)	$20,000	$2,000
other variable (10%)	$10,000	$1,000
Sales after Variable Expenses	$60,000	$6,000
Marketing Expense	$0	$0
Sales after Variable & Marketing	$60,000	$0
Fixed Expenses:		
employees	$20,000	$0
corner rent	$20,000	$0
other fixed	$10,000	$0
Profit after Variable & Fixed	$10,000	+$6,000

Unfortunately, Mary can't often grow sales without investing something. So how much would she be willing to invest to make an extra $10,000 in gross sales?

Theoretically, the maximum she would want to invest would be $6,000. That's the point at which her investment would be break-even. By investing an extra $6,000 in marketing she makes an extra $6,000 in net sales (sales after variable expenses). She would make $0 additional profit for the month, but at least she hasn't lost money.

$$\frac{\text{Net}}{\text{ROI}} = \frac{\text{Sales After Variable Expense}}{\text{Marketing Expense}} = \frac{\$6,000}{\$6,000} = 1.0$$

We've shown what this break-even investment looks like in P&L form below:

Mary's Lemonade Stand	Avg Month	Marketing Program
Gross Sales	$100,000	+$10,000
Variable Expenses:		
lemons (10%)	$10,000	$1,000
cups & other supplies (20%)	$20,000	$2,000
other variable (10%)	$10,000	$1,000
Sales after Variable Expenses	$60,000	$6,000
Marketing Expense	$0	**$6,000**
Sales after Variable & Marketing	$60,000	$0
Fixed Expenses:		
employees	$20,000	$0
corner rent	$20,000	$0
other fixed	$10,000	$0
Profit after Variable & Fixed	$10,000	$0

If we express all of our marketing programs in terms of ROI, it helps us to compare the impact of different marketing programs objectively by boiling them all down to a single comparable figure.

Let's say that Mary invested $6,000 in a radio advertisement which earned her the extra $10,000 in gross sales and $6,000 in net sales (the same as the previous break-even example.)

Several months later Mary has an opportunity to try something different. A billboard becomes available just above her lemonade stand To advertise on the billboard will cost $3,000. By advertising on the billboard, she earns an extra $8,000 in gross sales. This doesn't initially seem quite as good as the radio advertisement but she only had to invest half the amount to get it.

So which advertising opportunity was better? Which should she repeat if she has the opportunity?

In the billboard example, her Net ROI is better than break-even and is therefore better than the radio ad Net ROI. The calculation is shown below:

$$\frac{\text{Net}}{\text{ROI}} = \frac{\text{Sales After Variable Expense}}{\text{Marketing Expense}} = \frac{\$4,000}{\$3,000} = 1.33$$

Because the Net ROI is greater than 1.0, Mary will earn a profit on the billboard advertising investment. We compare the results of her two marketing efforts in a new P&L here:

Mary's Lemonade Stand	Avg Month	Radio Ad	Billboard Ad
Gross Sales	$100,000	+$10,000	+$8,000
Variable Expenses:			
lemons (10%)	$10,000	$1,000	$800
cups & other supplies (20%)	$20,000	$2,000	$1,600
other variable (10%)	$10,000	$1,000	$800
Sales after Variable Expenses	$60,000	$6,000	$4,800
Marketing Expense	$0	$6,000	$3,000
Sales after Variable & Marketing	$60,000	$0	$1,200
Fixed Expenses:			
employees	$20,000	$0	$0
corner rent	$20,000	$0	$0
other fixed	$10,000	$0	$0
Profit after Variable & Fixed	$10,000	$0	$1,200

From a gross sales perspective, Mary made more money from the radio advertisement than she did from the billboard, but from a Net ROI perspective, the billboard advertisement was a better investment.

Given this result, Mary may want to continue to invest in the billboard, hoping that these results repeat themselves over time. In fact, she may want to purchase additional billboard space around town. Unfortunately, there's no guarantee that other billboards will perform as well as this one did. Perhaps this one worked well because it was located directly above her stand and others located further away may do much worse. The only way that Mary can discover whether this is true is by testing another billboard and measuring the results.

Using this analysis, we may conclude that we should continue to invest in the billboard and perhaps never invest in radio advertising again. But something feels wrong with this analysis. The billboard advertisement may have earned more profit but it actually brought in fewer new customers than the radio advertisement. Said another way, the radio ad increased our topline and our new customers more than the billboard did. Is there any extra value to this and if so, how to we quantify it?

Lifetime Value

To answer these questions, we need to consider the long-term ROI of our marketing investment – not just the short-term Net ROI. To do so, we must realize that a new customer is worth more to your business than what you earn from them this month. In reality, each customer represents a potential lifetime stream of revenue to your business. This is why it may make sense for your marketing investment to break-even (Net ROI = 1.0) or even lose money (Net ROI < 1.0) in the short run to ensure a new long-term revenue stream.

To illustrate this, let's assume that you spend money on a marketing effort that brings in 100 new customers. We'll call these new customers "trialists." They were willing to try your business.

You'll earn the sales from these trialists relatively quickly as they respond to your marketing effort. And as we alluded to earlier, of those original 100 trialists, a good percentage may continue to do business with you, so that over time (sometimes many years) you continue to generate good revenue from these loyal customers. We'll call the trialists who like your business and continue to come in, loyalists.

So your marketing efforts generate immediate revenue and profits from 100 trialists in the short term. And your business continues to get sales and profits from a smaller group of loyalists over the long term. And there are typically customers who fall somewhere in-between. They're not exactly new loyal customers but they may come back on occasion.

We've highlighted this idea with a simple visual depiction.

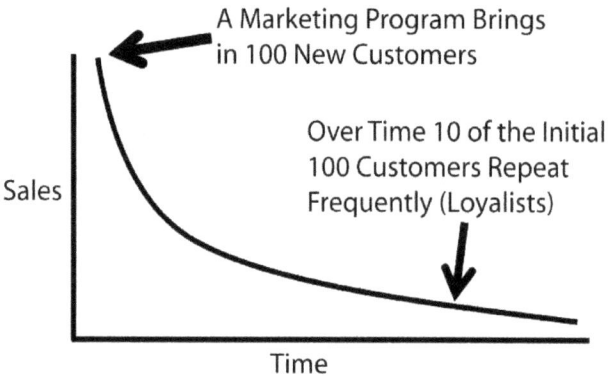

Because of this long-term effect, a more accurate way of determining whether your marketing expense pays back over the long-run is to factor in the "lifetime value" of the extra customers you've obtained.

Doing this is not particularly easy. Our graph helps to illustrate the idea but the initial trial rate, relevant time period, loyalist conversion rate, revenue and other factors can vary greatly depending on your business. To figure out how much an average customer is worth to you, consider the following:

- How long does the average customer continue to do business with you and how does their expenditure change with time? Does this purchase rate tend to increase or decrease with time, or is there a more complicated life cycle?

- What percentage of your customers are loyalists representing the greatest revenue per person? Any given marketing effort may have the potential to generate roughly the same percentage of new loyalists.

- How much revenue do you take in on average from a single transaction and how much revenue do you take in per year from a very good customer or loyalist?

You may have a sense for these types of things, or you may not. If you don't, it may be worth making some rough assumptions to aid you in determining the Net ROI of your marketing spend taking lifetime value into account. We'll call this the lifetime ROI.

Let's revisit the radio advertising break-even example for Mary's Lemonade Stand:

$$\frac{\text{Net}}{\text{ROI}} = \frac{\text{Sales After Variable Expense}}{\text{Marketing Expense}} = \frac{\$6,000}{\$6,000} = 1.0$$

Let's assume the extra revenue resulted from one thousand people all purchasing lemonade for $10 each on average. (Let's also assume this is some very premium lemonade!) Now, let's also assume that, on average, 50 percent of Mary's customers return to her stand and purchase an extra glass of lemonade at some time over the course of the summer. This means that in gross sales terms:

$$\text{Immediate Return from Marketing} = 1{,}000 \text{ Customers} \times \$10 = \mathbf{\$10{,}000}$$

$$+ \text{ Repeat Business} = 500 \text{ Customers} \times \$10 = \mathbf{\$5{,}000}$$

$$= \text{Lifetime Return from Marketing} \qquad \mathbf{\$15{,}000}$$

We can add this result in a new column in our profit and loss statement, next to the column where we calculated immediate return from marketing earlier. Now we have a P&L statement that shows a normal month (column 1), a month in which we invested $10,000 in marketing (column 2), and the return on that marketing investment over the long-run (column 3).

Mary's Lemonade Stand	Avg Month	Marketing Program	Lifetime Calc
Gross Sales	$100,000	$10,000	$15,000
Variable Expenses:			
lemons (10%)	$10,000	$1,000	$1,500
cups & other supplies (20%)	$20,000	$2,000	$3,000
other variable (10%)	$10,000	$1,000	$1,500
Sales after Variable Expenses	$60,000	$6,000	$9,000
Marketing Expense	$0	**$6,000**	**$6,000**
Sales after Variable & Marketing	$60,000	$0	$3,000
Fixed Expenses:			
employees	$20,000	$0	$0
corner rent	$20,000	$0	$0
other fixed	$10,000	$0	$0
Profit after Variable & Fixed	$10,000	$0	$3,000

We calculate lifetime ROI in the same way that we calculate Net ROI:

$$\frac{\text{Lifetime}}{\text{ROI}} = \frac{\text{Lifetime Sales After Variable Expense}}{\text{Marketing Expense}}$$

In this example, Mary spent \$6,000 in marketing expenses which earned her an incremental net sales \$9,000 in lifetime value for a total lifetime Net ROI of \$9,000 divided by \$6000 or 1.5.

$$\frac{\text{Lifetime}}{\text{ROI}} = \frac{\begin{array}{c}\text{Lifetime Sales After}\\ \text{Variable Expense}\end{array}}{\text{Marketing Expense}} = \frac{\$9,000}{\$6,000} = 1.5$$

So, after taking the lifetime value of a customer into account, Mary has calculated that her ROI increases from 1.0 (or breakeven) to 1.5, meaning she will earn an incremental \$3,000 profit over time as a result of her initial marketing expenditure.

Let's return to our initial question about whether the investment in radio or billboard advertising was a better long-term investment for Mary.

Mary's Lemonade Stand	Avg Month	Radio Ad Lifetime	Billboard Ad Lifetime
Gross Sales	$100,000	+$15,000	+$12,000
Variable Expenses:			
lemons (10%)	$10,000	$1,500	$1,200
cups & other supplies (20%)	$20,000	$3,000	$2,400
other variable (10%)	$10,000	$1,500	$1,200
Sales after Variable Expenses	$60,000	$9,000	$7,200
Marketing Expense	$0	**$6,000**	**$3,000**
Sales after Variable & Marketing	$60,000	$3,000	$1,200
Fixed Expenses:			
employees	$20,000	$0	$0
corner rent	$20,000	$0	$0
other fixed	$10,000	$0	$0
Profit after Variable & Fixed	$10,000	$3,000	$1,200

Now things have become a bit more complicated! In the short-run, Mary made more profit from the billboard advertisement than she did from radio. However, because the radio advertisement brought in more customers who will pay her more over the long-run, the radio ad was a better long-term investment.

As a business owner who needs to pay the bills every month a lifetime value can seem hypothetical at best. But think about it another way. Very few marketing investments pay back in one month or even over the course of several months. If you invest in only those activities that pay back immediately, you may miss out on an opportunity to grow your business more significantly in the long-run.

Marketing is both an immediate payback vehicle and a long term investment. Learning to calculate both the immediate net ROI and the lifetime value ROI will help you to better evaluate the value of that investment now and in the long-run.

Determining Return Before You Invest

It's important to measure the success of a marketing vehicle after you've invested in it, but how do you determine how much to invest in something for the first time? Suppose it will cost you $5,000 to place an ad in a local magazine. Will it be worth the investment?

First, let's separate the question of whether the investment makes sense for your business from the question of whether you're paying too much for the advertisement.

Many resources exist that can help you determine if what you're paying is fair. Many common advertising vehicles have published their ad rates, although as we've discussed these are often merely starting points for negotiations. You may be successful in bringing them down by 10 or 20% (but often not as much as 50%). If the advertising vehicle is a mature source that's been around for a while, these market rates are typically pretty representative of what the market will bear. You can also discuss the advertising vehicle with other members of the business community that may have invested themselves. Finally, if you utilize an advertising agency to negotiate on your behalf, you'll benefit from a resource that understands what type of discount you may expect and how this will vary based on factors like available inventory, time of year, etc.

Once you've determined that the advertising expense is reflective of what others have paid, the vehicle itself may still be too expensive for you. This isn't simply a matter of the absolute investment amount. The bigger issue is whether you can expect to reach the right types of people and whether those people will respond to the advertisement.

You'll need to do a rough estimate for the return you can expect by multiplying the number of people who will see the ad, by the expected response rate (it will typically be a very low number – often below 1%), and multiply this by the expected revenue per person.

Reach (people who see the ad)
x
Response Rate
x
Revenue Per Response
―――――――――――――
= Total Expected Return

And that total expected return should be less than what you're willing to pay to advertise.

The people who have sold you an advertisement should be able to tell you how many people will see it. This is called "reach." Some advertisers know this number better than others. A magazine should know what its distribution is, but the owner of a billboard may have a more difficult time calculating how many cars drive by on an average day. Every advertiser will give you a number but it's your responsibility to apply a bit of common sense to determine if it seems accurate.

And "reach" isn't the only number that's important. Also consider whether people truly "see" the advertisement or not. Someone selling you space on the side of the bus will tell you how many people the bus drives by on an average day. But of these people, how many truly see your advertisement? Commuters are often paying attention to other things. On the other hand, people will often listen to a radio advertisement simply because they like the station and haven't bothered or are unable to change the channel. This is a concept known as engagement. Low engagement vehicles (like busses) should be much cheaper per person that "sees" the ad than higher engagement vehicles like radio or online advertising.

Once you determine how many people will see the advertisement, how do you guess what the response rate will be? History will be your best guide. If you've ever advertised in any other vehicle, and you've estimated results using the methods described in this chapter, you should have some sense for response, assuming you know what type of revenue you get from your average customer.

Using a bit of algebra, we can determine from what we already know and from making an adjustment to the expected return calculation presented earlier:

$$\frac{\text{Response}}{\text{Rate}} = \frac{\text{Total return (Absolute)}}{\text{Reach x Revenue per Person}}$$

If, for example, you advertised in a magazine with a circulation of 50,000 people and you were reasonably certain that a sales rise in that period of $2,000 was as a result of this ad, and you knew that your average revenue per person per month was about $100, you can calculate response rate. Total return ($2,000) divided by reach (50,000) times revenue per person ($100) yields a response rate of 0.04% (0.00004)

Wow! Are response rates really this low? The short answer is yes. Many mass market vehicles reach lots and lots of consumers but, as we've mentioned, only a few of them may actually respond to your ad. Either they won't be a good fit for your offering, or they weren't paying attention, or it was a bad time, or any of a thousand different excuses. This is the way the advertising world works and it's why it may seem as if you're getting a great deal when you advertise on television with an ad that reaches many thousands of people.

This response rate isn't a particularly interesting number by itself. It's really only useful as a means of determining what you may expect to get in return for your advertising spend, or as a means of comparing different advertising vehicles. You can imagine that guessing such a tiny number might be very difficult without another example. If you had guessed something like a 0.08% response rate, it might seem as if you'd somehow miraculously managed to guess something very similar to the actual rate, but note that this is still double the actual rate, and would result in you being willing to spend twice the amount on the advertisement.

Because response rates are so difficult to guess, many advertisers take a small risk and invest in new advertising vehicles in order to measure results for themselves. Once you've determined what to expect, you can make a larger investment in the future if warranted by the results.

A Note on Seasonal Businesses

If your business is seasonal, you may have considered advertising during the off-season in an attempt to even out your sales. This may or may not make sense. If customers are less likely to spend during the off-season, then your advertising expenditure may attract fewer customers overall, because the underlying base of potential customers is lower.

For example, if you typically get one thousand customers per month during the season and five hundred per month during the off season, then a 10% increase will give you an extra one hundred customers during the season but only fifty during the off-season. If your advertising expenditure is the same regardless of the season, then your ROI will be much lower during the off-season.

You may want to bring in additional customers to offset your fixed costs during the off-season, but this will make sense only if you've found a marketing expense that pays back at greater than 1.0. Remember that we calculate the return on marketing expense (which is variable) against variable costs only. Marketing will help offset fixed costs only if your return is higher than the difference between the marketing expense and your variable costs. If you've calculated an ROI during the good season and you know that a particular marketing expense pays greater than 1.0, you still have to consider the possibility that the same marketing effort will be less effective in the off-season. Using the above example, if marketing is half as effective in the off-season, you will be able to defray fixed costs only if your net marketing ROI is 2.0 or greater during your good season.

You may be better off attempting to reduce your fixed costs (if possible) during the off-season than assuming that marketing will help you offset your fixed costs. Before investing, do a hypothetical calculation yourself.

Measuring Results Summary

- Before spending a dime on marketing tactics, ensure that you know who your target audience is and can clearly articulate your primary message.

- To determine the results of a particular program, start by determining your baseline level of sales and determine that the incremental results you saw during the promotion were in fact a result of that promotion and not something else. To do this, you can include a coupon or some other means of measurement with a specific promotion, or simply ask new customers how they heard about you.

- A Net ROI is a good way of measuring the payback on a particular program and of comparing one program to another. Net ROI is calculated by dividing the full cost of the marketing program by the additional variable expenses that you need to pay to service the incremental customers obtained through the program.

- You can enhance your ROI calculation by including the idea of lifetime value. This takes into account the idea that a customer is worth more than he or she pays during the single period in which you're measuring your results.

16

CONCLUSION

There are thousands of potential customers out there. And there are countless ways to reach them and many things that you might say to convince them to purchase from you. It's easy to become overwhelmed and simply choose to do what you've always done, or to do nothing at all.

The key elements of success are to ensure that you know who to talk to and where and how to find them (targeting), ensure that you're saying the one or two things that are most likely to convince them to buy from you (messaging), and to select the vehicles that enable you to reach your target most effectively and cost-efficiently (tactics).

Take some time to understand who your existing customers are. Talk to them or conduct a formal survey that will help you find more people just like them. Understand who lives and works in the area immediately surrounding your business using online zip code search tools. If you're just starting a business talk to the customers of an established business that looks most similar to the one you want to start.

Once you know a bit more about the types of people you'd like to attract, spend some time considering what you'd like to say. Ensure that your message tells people how you are different than your competition. Be honest and highlight your strengths. Don't try to be something you are not. If you do, you'll only disappoint the potential customers who value what you claim to provide, and they'll share their disappointment with others. The customers who value what you do well will pay for your expertise. And they'll be satisfied with the results and tell others about you. Once you've found a message that is crisp, clear, and differentiated, be consistent. Don't try to follow every new trend. Your message will become part of your brand and should stay consistent for years.

We've mentioned many tactics in this book. Not all of them will be right for you. Using the information you've obtained here and your best judgment, try one of two of them this quarter and measure your results. The following quarter (or next year), continue doing what has worked the best and test a few more ideas. In this way, you'll end up spending money on the very best and most profitable ways to reach your target audience.

We hope that this book has provided you with important insights into the art and science of marketing which enable you to focus and achieve results.

Because resources change so quickly, we have avoided listing specific resources in this book (with the exception of general tactics). For more information and for links to specific resources visit us online at FadFreeMarketing.com. We continue to research new offerings and we do so independently. The resources that we link to have not paid us to provide links. Our goal is to provide you with a few real-world offerings that we believe can truly help. And we encourage you to share examples of what has and has not worked for you so that others in the business community can benefit from your experience.

Best of luck, and keep optimizing!

ABOUT THE AUTHOR

Bryan Duke has engaged his passion for marketing as both an entrepreneur and as a brand and marketing manager in fortune 500 companies such as Procter & Gamble, America Online and Novartis. He has consulted with companies both large and small on projects ranging from target audience refinement, messaging and advertising development, and forecasting and results measurement.

In addition, he has run numerous training courses, participated in educational seminars, and blogs a bit in his spare time. Bryan has been recognized for his ability to present marketing fundamentals clearly, carefully choosing the 20% of issues that deliver 80% of the impact. He is an advocate of continuous testing and measurement principles that enable sustained growth in ROI and profit.

This broad range of experience has given him a good sense for what does and does not work in the real world and a finely tuned BS meter.

www.FadFreeMarketing.com